C000192539

Roya South
Norman.

THE HAPPIEST DAYS
OF YOUR LIFE

A Farce in Three Acts

by

JOHN DIGHTON

SAMUEL FRENCH

LONDON

NEW YORK   TORONTO   SYDNEY   HOLLYWOOD

© 1949 IN VOL. "PLAYS OF THE YEAR 1948-49",
BY PAUL ELEK PUBLISHERS LTD

© 1951 BY SAMUEL FRENCH LTD

1. *This play is fully protected under the Copyright Laws of the British Commonwealth of Nations, the United States of America and all countries of the Berne and Universal Copyright Conventions.*

2. *All rights, including Stage, Motion Picture, Radio, Television, Public Reading, and Translation into Foreign Languages, are strictly reserved.*

3. **No part of this publication may lawfully be reproduced in ANY form or by any means—photocopying, typescript, recording (including video-recording), manuscript, electronic, mechanical, or otherwise—or be transmitted or stored in a retrieval system, without prior permission.**

4. Rights of Performance by Amateurs are controlled by SAMUEL FRENCH LTD, 52 FITZROY STREET, LONDON W1P 6JR, and they, or their authorized agents, issue licences to amateurs on payment of a fee. **It is an infringement of the Copyright to give any performance or public reading of the play before the fee has been paid and the licence issued.**

5. Licences are issued subject to the understanding that it shall be made clear in all advertising matter that the audience will witness an amateur performance; that the names of the authors of the plays shall be included on all announcements and on all programmes; and that the integrity of the author's work will be preserved.

    The Royalty Fee indicated below is subject to contract and subject to variation at the sole discretion of Samuel French Ltd.

    Basic fee for each and every
    performance by amateurs   Code M
    in the British Isles

    In Theatres or Halls seating Six Hundred or more the fee will be subject to negotiation.

    In Territories Overseas the fee quoted above may not apply. A fee will be quoted on application to our local authorized agent, or if there is no such agent, on application to Samuel French Ltd, London.

    The publication of this play does not imply that it is necessarily available for performance by amateurs or professionals, either in the British Isles or Overseas. Amateurs intending production must, in their own interests, make application to Samuel French Ltd or their agents for consent before starting rehearsals or booking a theatre or hall.

ISBN 0 573 01169 9

THE HAPPIEST DAYS OF YOUR LIFE

Produced at the Apollo Theatre, London, on the 29th March, 1948, with the following cast of characters—

(in the order of their appearance)

DICK TASSELL, Assistant Master at Hilary Hall	*Myles Eason*
RAINBOW, School Porter and Groundsman	*Douglas Ives*
RUPERT BILLINGS, Senior Assistant Master at Hilary Hall	*Colin Gordon*
GODFREY POND, Headmaster of Hilary Hall	*George Howe*
MISS EVELYN WHITCHURCH, Principal of St Swithins School for Girls	*Margaret Rutherford*
MISS GOSSAGE, Senior Assistant Mistress at St. Swithins	*Viola Lyel*
HOPCROFT MI., Pupil at Hilary Hall	*Peter Davies*
BARBARA CAHOUN, Pupil at St Swithins	*Molly Weir*
JOYCE HARPER, Assistant Mistress at St. Swithins	*Patricia Hastings*
THE REVEREND EDWARD PECK	*Stringer Davis*
MRS PECK, his wife	*Betty Woolfe*
EDGAR SOWTER	*Douglas Stewart*
MRS SOWTHER, his wife	*Irene Relph*

The Play directed by RICHARD BIRD

SYNOPSIS OF SCENES

The action of the play passes in the Masters' Common Room at Hilary Hall School for Boys, in Hampshire

ACT I

The first day of the Summer term. Afternoon

ACT II

Saturday afternoon. Three weeks later

ACT III

Two hours later

THE HAPPIEST DAYS OF YOUR LIFE

ACT I

SCENE—*The Masters' Common Room at Hilary Hall School for Boys, in Hampshire. The first day of the Summer term, about 4 p.m.*

The room is furnished with the typical austerity of its kind. Up LC *at the back are french windows with corner seats and heavy curtains, opening on to a terrace with a view of the school grounds beyond. Up* R *at the back are double doors, which lead to the hall, where the staircase, lit by two windows, winds up and out of sight* L *to* R. *A passage below the staircase leads off* R *to the boys' part of the building. The fireplace is* C *of the wall* R, *and down stage* L *a door, over which hangs a map of the world, leads to the Headmaster's study. A heavy oak refectory table dominates the centre of the room. There are elbow chairs* R *and* L *of the table and a dining-room chair above it. There is a moderately comfortable easy chair upstage of the fireplace, and another to* R *of the french windows. There is a row of four hat pegs, on one of which hangs the Headmaster's mortar-board, on the wall* L, *between the study door and the french windows. Beneath the pegs stands a dining-room chair. There are two small lockers for personal belongings, on the* R *wall, above and below the fireplace. A well-filled bookcase, with three silver cups on the top, stands between the french windows and the double doors. Underneath the downstage locker* R *is a small table with a telephone on a long flex, and some old magazines. By it stand a waste-paper basket and a stool. Above the fireplace there is another small table with a geographical globe on it. A marble clock and two bronze figures carrying candles with shades, stand on the mantelpiece, over which hangs an oil painting of a Victorian gentleman. A brass fender with fire-irons, and a rug in front of the fireplace, complete the furniture in the room. In the hall, above the* L *double door, is a small table. The school bell stands on the sill of the first window, and the school notice board hangs on the wall between the windows.*

(See the Ground Plan at the end of the Play.)

When the CURTAIN *rises the stage is empty. The* R *side of the french windows is open, and the sun is shining brilliantly. The double doors are closed but the Common Room, if not luxurious, looks bright and airy. After a moment the double doors are barged open from outside and* DICK TASSELL *enters. He is a tall, cheerful young man of about twenty-six, hatless and wearing a sports jacket and grey flannel trousers. He has had to shoulder the doors open, as he is laden with a suitcase, a cricket bag, a bag of golf clubs, a tennis racquet and a net bag of tennis balls. He staggers with all these to the table* C *and drops everything on it. He looks*

I

*around him with an air of resignation, then turning, moves to the double
doors and calls.*

Tassell (*calling*) Rainbow. (*He moves to the locker above the fireplace, opens it and glances in. He is surprised and pleased at what he sees*)
Good Lord! (*He pulls out a dusty-looking mortar-board and gown. He
blows the dust off the mortar-board, puts it on to avoid holding it, and
moving down* R *starts to shake the gown*)

(Rainbow *comes down the stairs and enters the room. He is a
gloomy-eyed man of middle age. Employed as school porter-cum-
groundsman, he achieves a compromise by wearing a porter's trousers and
waistcoat but no tunic. He carries a duster. His tone of voice matches
his lugubrious expression*)

(*In a friendly tone*) Hullo, Rainbow.
Rainbow (*gloomy but pleased*) Mr Tassell. (*He moves* L *of* Tassell
and shakes hands with him) Well, well. Very pleased to see you back,
sir.
Tassell (*wryly*) Not so sure that I am. After being airborne
for five years, I'm afraid I'm going to find Hilary Hall a bit slow.
(*He points to his luggage*) I just want a thing or two out of these,
then you can take them up. (*He looks around reminiscently*) Five
years. (*He looks at Rainbow*) You don't look a day older. (*He crosses
below the table to the hat pegs, looking at the gown*) A bit moth-eaten,
that's all.
Rainbow. Eh?
Tassell (*indicating the gown*) This. Never expected to find it
still in my old locker. (*He takes off the mortar-board and hangs it with
the gown on one of the pegs*)
Rainbow (*shaking his head*) The school was evacuated, soon
after you'd gone. Only come back this term.
Tassell (*moving above the table* C *and opening the cricket bag*) Gosh,
you've had a long holiday. (*He takes a pair of white cricket boots out
of the bag and places them on the table* C)
Rainbow (*moving* R *of Tassell; lugubriously*) Holiday—I've had
mice in the music-room, dry-rot in one of the class-rooms, and
beetles all over my basement.
Tassell. Sounds most unpleasant. (*He grins resignedly*) Same
old Rainbow, can see that, and same old Hilary Hall. Might as
well get used to it, I suppose. (*He rummages in the cricket bag*)
Rainbow (*mysteriously*) The same, yet not the same.
Tassell (*looking up*) Mm?
Rainbow. It won't be what it was—whatever it possibly may
be, perhaps.
Tassell (*confused*) Say that again. (*He takes a cricket bat from the
bag*)
Rainbow (*profoundly*) Mark my words—two into one won't go.
It isn't feasible.

Tassell (*moving with the bat below the table* c) What the hell are you talking about? (*He makes some practice strokes with the bat*)

Rainbow. I'm sorry, Mr Tassell—but I can't go over the head of the Head.

Tassell (*leaning on the table* c) Sounds to me as if you'd gone off the head of the head.

Rainbow (*moving below the table* c *to* R *of Tassell*) I'm telling you confidential, he says to me.

Tassell (*placing the bat on the table* c) Who says?

Rainbow. Mr Pond says.

Tassell (*enlightened*) Oh—and you can't go over Mr Pond's head. (*He eases* L)

Rainbow (*patiently*) The Head's head, that's what I said.

(Rupert Billings *comes down the stairs and enters the room. He is in the thirties, has a cynical disposition and a dry way of talking. He is carrying an armful of books, a folded woollen scarf in the Hilary Hall colours of red and yellow, a mortar-board and gown and a folding leather frame with four photographs in it*)

Billings (*as he enters*) I say, Rainbow, my bedroom door's locked.

Tassell (*easing down* L) Hullo, R.B.

Billings (*pleased to see Tassell*) So the prodigal son is home again. (*Still laden, he crosses to Tassell and endeavours to shake hands with him*) I thought I heard a faint whisper of your arrival. (*He turns to Rainbow*) You might unlock it when you go up, and take my cases in. (*He puts the books, mortar-board and photograph frame on the table* c) I left 'em on the landing. (*To Tassell*) Well, how are you? No, don't tell me; (*he puts the gown and scarf on the table*) we'll save all that for the long summer evenings. (*He picks up the bag of tennis balls*) The weapons of peace once more. Glad to see you're well armed. (*He replaces the bag of balls on the table and picks up some of his books*)

Tassell. I suppose you've been taking games in my absence?

Billings (*crossing with the books to the locker below the fireplace; dryly*) I have. For that reason—if no other—I'm delighted to see you back.

Tassell (*moving to the french windows; to Rainbow*) How's the pitch, by the way?

Rainbow (*moving above the table* c) It's all right now. What it'll be in a week's time it's not for me to say.

(Billings, *before opening the locker, puts his books down for a moment or two on the table below it, and glances at an article in one of the magazines*)

Tassell (*glancing out of the window*) The weather looks all right to me.

Rainbow (*shaking his head*) It's the other I'm referring to. (*He picks up Tassell's suitcase and cricket bag*) Grass needs a rest, same as we do. After all—it's only human.

(RAINBOW *shakes his head again, moves into the hall, carries the case and bag upstairs and exits.* TASSELL *looks after him curiously, then moves to the double doors and closes them.* BILLINGS *puts down the magazine, opens the locker and puts his books in it*)

TASSELL (*moving above the* L *end of the table* C) You know, I think old Rainbow's beginning to go at the edges.

BILLINGS. Nothing to go. (*He takes a pair of boxing-gloves out of the locker and looks at them in surprise*) How the devil did those get in there?

TASSELL. You confiscated them from Hopcroft last term—my last term, I mean.

BILLINGS (*remembering*) So I did. Five years ago. (*He moves above the table* C) You've got a memory. Little blighter was wearing them in chapel—for a bet. (*He drops the gloves on the table* C)

TASSELL. He's been saying the most extraordinary things.

BILLINGS. Hopcroft?

TASSELL. No—Rainbow. Seems to think something funny's going to happen here.

BILLINGS (*picking up the remainder of his books*) Be the first time it ever has. (*He moves to his locker*)

TASSELL (*picking up his bag of golf clubs*) Hopcroft's left by now, I suppose? (*He leans the golf bag against the back of the easy chair above the fireplace*)

BILLINGS (*placing the books in his locker*) Yes. But his brother's here—Hopcroft Mi. The same thing, only a good deal worse. (*He brings the remains of a stick of pink rock out of his locker*) Ugh!

TASSELL (*moving to the table* C) What's that? Another pre-war confiscation? (*He picks up the boxing-gloves and slings them into the easy chair above the fireplace*)

BILLINGS. Yes. (*He licks his sticky fingers, about to return the rock to the locker*) Oh, it's one of my favourites. (*He puts the rock in his jacket pocket*)

TASSELL (*sitting in the chair* R *of the table* C) Thirteen weeks in the heart of darkest Hampshire. First term back seems a bit of a grisly prospect.

BILLINGS (*moving to the table and picking up his mortar-board and gown*) You should have been with us for the last fifteen terms. (*He takes the mortar-board and gown to the pegs* L)

TASSELL. Yes, Rainbow said you'd been evacuated.

BILLINGS (*hanging the mortar-board and gown on the pegs*) That's putting it mildly. We were moved three times. The first was a boarding-house—St. Moritz.

TASSELL (*surprised*) Switzerland?

BILLINGS (*turning*) No, Swiss Cottage. We then went to share a **veterinary** college.

TASSELL. You mean with a whole lot of animals?

BILLINGS. Yes, but to prevent any misunderstanding we were always referred to as their honoured guests. We ended up in a disused fire-station near Ludlow. Up the pole to bed every night. (*He wanders up to the french windows*) Thank Heaven to be back in Hampshire. (*He steps just outside the window and looks around*)

TASSELL. Well, I don't know. Twelve miles to the nearest flick, forty to a theatre.

(BILLINGS *turns and re-enters*)

And as for feminine society—nil.

BILLINGS. There's always Mrs Hampstead.

TASSELL. Mrs Hampstead may be the matron of this school, but she's certainly not feminine. Female possibly, but feminine certainly not. Damn it, she's got an R.A.F. moustache.

BILLINGS (*moving L of the table C*) Better known as Hampstead Heath. Yes, there is that, I admit.

TASSELL. It's all very well for you—you hate women, anyway.

BILLINGS. If you had to live with four aunts, all wanting to mother you . . . Look what they've done this time. (*He moves below the table C, picks up the scarf and lets it unroll. It is about ten feet long*)

TASSELL (*rising*) Great Scott! (*He picks up the end of the scarf and helps Billings roughly roll it up*)

BILLINGS (*eyeing the scarf gloomily*) They did a yard each.

TASSELL. A little warm, isn't it, for the summer term? (*He picks up the photograph frame and looks at it*)

BILLINGS. They were knitting it for next winter, but I stopped them at the end of the March quarter. (*He puts the scarf on the table C*)

TASSELL (*indicating the photograph frame*) This is new, isn't it? The portrait gallery?

BILLINGS (*sadly*) Last birthday. And they always make sure I pack it.

TASSELL (*looking at the photographs*) So this is the Big Four. (*He opens the frame and stands it on the table C, facing the audience*)

BILLINGS (*picking up the cricket bat and using the handle as a pointer*) Reading from left to right. Aunts Flora, Nora, Dora, and Auntie Ethel.

TASSELL. Why Ethel?

BILLINGS. I don't think my grandmother expected her. (*He puts the bat on the table*)

(POND *enters down L. He is a small, pompous man of about fifty, dressed in a dark suit, and wearing his gown. He is carrying a letter, a telegram, some school lists and a notebook*)

POND. Ah—good afternoon, gentlemen.

BILLINGS. 'Afternoon, Headmaster.

Pond (*shaking hands with Billings and then with Tassell*) Return of the warrior? Splendid. (*He pats Tassell on the shoulder*) And delighted to be back in harness, I've no doubt.

Tassell. Oh yes, rather.

(Billings *eyes Tassell dryly*)

Pond. Capital. (*He crosses Billings to the pegs, takes down his mortar-board and dons it*) We have all pulled together in the past. I am sure we shall continue to do so (*he moves down* L) in the circumstances about to prevail.

Billings. In the what?

Pond. Of—of course, you haven't heard the news. It was very sudden indeed. In fact I've had no time to inform the parents as yet.

(Billings *moves to* L *of Tassell below the table* C *and folds up the photograph frame*)

Tassell. Nothing bad, sir, I hope?

Pond. No, no—inconvenient, shall we say? No more. (*He opens out the letter*) I received the following two days ago from the Ministry of Devacuation. (*He reads*) "Dear Sir." (*He stops and looks at Billings and Tassell*) Sit down.

(Tassell *sits on the arm of the chair* R *of the table* C, *and* Billings *perches himself on the front edge of the table* C)

(*He resumes reading*) "Under the Emergency Powers Act, nineteen forty, Sub-section three, para. fifteen—Schools, Boarding and Private, Elementary and Preparatory, Secondary, Kindergarten and Grammar—this Ministry is empowered to allocate educational premises. Some schools returning from evacuation have, unfortunately, lost their original buildings, and it has become unavoidably necessary to ask you to share your own with another school of similar size and type. You will receive a further communication in due course. Your obedient servant, C. C. Fraphampton, Deputy Sub-Controller of Premises, Schools Division."

(Billings *and* Tassell *rise*)

Tassell. So that's what Rainbow was blithering about—two into one won't go——

Pond. You know what these Ministries are—their yea is yea and their nay is nay.

Billings (*easing* L *of the chair* L *of the table*) In due course, he says, doesn't he? That's probably two or three years. Very likely it'll never happen.

Pond (*crossing below the* L *end of the table* C) It *has* happened. (*He puts the Ministry letter and the school lists on the* L *end of the table* C) Yesterday afternoon this wire came from Hastings. (*He reads the telegram*) "Staff and pupils arriving four-fifteen tomorrow. Whitchurch, Principal of St Swithins." (*He hands Billings the telegram to look at*)

TASSELL (*curiously*) St Swithins——

BILLINGS. Now I suppose it'll rain for forty days.

POND (*taking the telegram back from Billings; severely*) This is hardly the time for Fourth Form humour, Billings. (*He glances again at the telegram*) Staff and pupils at four-fifteen. (*He crosses below Tassell to the fireplace and stands with his back to it*) That's only a few minutes after our own boys arrive. Before then, we've got to get everything settled. Accommodation, of course, will be the principal problem. Perhaps one of you'd take down the details——

(BILLINGS *signs to Tassell to do it*)

Billings.

(BILLINGS *crosses below Tassell to Pond*)

(*He gives the notebook to Billings*) Now, to start with—sleeping quarters.

(BILLINGS *takes a pencil out of Tassell's breast pocket.* TASSELL *perches himself on the* R *end of the table* C)

(*To Billings*) I propose to put you in Mrs Hampstead's room.

BILLINGS (*outraged*) What!

(TASSELL *grins*)

POND. You and Tassell.

(TASSELL *rises in horror*)

It's a large airy room——

BILLINGS. Yes, and she's a large hairy woman——

POND. Mrs Hampstead's peculiarities are neither here nor there.

BILLINGS. They may not be here, but they will be there.

TASSELL. Surely we shan't be as overcrowded as all that?

POND. It will be a severe squeeze for everyone.

BILLINGS. Well, I refuse to do any squeezing in Mrs Hampstead's room. (*He thrusts the notebook into Tassell's hands*) I'd rather go back to my aunts. (*He turns and moves up stage to the double doors*)

POND (*catching Billings and hurrying him back; pained*) Billings, if you're going to be unreasonable from the start——

(TASSELL *perches himself on the* R *end of the table* C)

BILLINGS. Unreasonable—— (*He puts the pencil in his breast pocket*)

POND. Mrs Hampstead agreed most readily.

BILLINGS. Oh—did she?

POND. She made no difficulties whatever about moving into your room.

BILLINGS. Into mine? (*He understands*) Oh. Objection overruled.

TASSELL. Same here.

POND (*eyeing them reprovingly*) We must try to remember that we are the hosts on this occasion. St Swithins are our honoured guests. Kindly bear that in mind.

BILLINGS (*to Tassell; ominously*) Honoured guests.

POND (*crossing below the table* C *to* L) Now—we've got Matron in your room, and you two in hers. (*To Tassell*) Make a note of that.

(TASSELL *takes his pencil back from Billings' breast pocket and makes an entry in the notebook*)

That leaves Tassell's room free for the St Swithins staff.

TASSELL. They'll certainly have a squeeze.

POND (*correcting himself*) For one of their staff. I'm not quite certain about the rest. (*He puts his hands behind him, bunches up his gown, moves to the french windows and stands looking out*) There are no more rooms in the staff wing——

BILLINGS (*moving above the table* C; *casually*) Except yours, of course.

POND (*turning his head; taken aback*) Mine?

BILLINGS. It's the largest and airiest of the lot. Quite a few of them could sleep with you in there.

POND. Not with someone in my position.

BILLINGS (*curiously*) What position d'you sleep in?

POND (*dropping his bunched-up gown and turning*) My position as Headmaster. (*He moves down* L)

TASSELL. Well, perhaps you could just share with their Head-master—Whitechapel, or whatever his name is?

POND (*picking up a few of his lists from the* L *end of the table* C; *firmly*) I suggest we leave the question of my room for the moment. We must avoid favouritism at all costs. I hope that's quite clear?

BILLINGS (*crossing to the stool down* R) Clear as crystal. (*He sits, takes the stick of rock from his pocket and surreptitiously starts chewing it*)

POND. Good. Well then—it occurred to me we could probably sleep most of their masters in the carpenter's shop—— How does that strike you?

TASSELL. I think you've hit the nail on the head, Head.

BILLINGS. Convenient, too—they could make their beds and then lie on them.

POND (*crossing to the fireplace; dryly*) There will be no shortage of beds. (*He turns*) We have all those camp ones in the loft. We can set . . . (*He half catches Billings sucking the rock and stops speaking*)

(BILLINGS *looks up and hastily hides the rock*)

(*He resumes*) We can set up the requisite number in the carpenter's shop and the remainder will do for the boys.

BILLINGS (*surprised*) Our boys?

POND. No, no—theirs, naturally. (*He moves a little up* R)

(BILLINGS *takes a bite of rock*)

(*He turns suddenly*) The only question . . . (*He sees the rock*) Give me that. (*He moves to Billings, takes the rock, and puts it in his jacket pocket*) The only question is where to put them. Our boys could give up one of the dormitories, I suppose——

BILLINGS. Seems a pity to move them.

POND (*with his hands in his jacket pockets, moving thoughtfully up* R) Just what I was thinking. But where else could they go? There isn't anywhere.

BILLINGS. That passage in C wing is fairly wide, and there are doors at both ends.

POND (*taking the rock from his pocket*) So there are. Excellent idea. (*He absent-mindedly takes a bite of rock*)

(BILLINGS *sees him do it.* POND *hastily puts the rock behind his back*)

TASSELL (*mildly surprised*) C wing? Outside the stinks room, d'you mean?

POND (*speaking as if his mouth is full of rock*) Don't be irrelevant, Tassell, please. If the passage in question runs past the scientific laboratories, what of it? It may be a little (*he removes a piece of rock from his teeth with one finger*) awkward for our science classes, but we must put up with these things.

BILLINGS (*to Tassell*) After all, St Swithins are our honoured guests.

TASSELL (*making entries in the notebook*) "Masters—carpenter's shop. Boys—passage outside stinks."

BILLINGS. Any over can always sleep inside.

POND. That's true.

TASSELL (*sarcastically*) And I suppose they can all use the sinks as wash-basins.

POND. Which sinks?

TASSELL. The sinks in the stinks.

POND. So they can. I'm glad you thought of that. I was afraid they might have to do without. (*He moves* L *of the table* C, *puts the rock on the tennis racquet and wipes his fingers on Billing.' scarf*) So much for sleeping quarters. Now for meals. As far as I can see, Cook will simply have to stagger them.

BILLINGS. That won't be difficult.

TASSELL (*to Pond*) I don't quite follow, sir.

POND. Simple enough. We shall have a first and second service.

TASSELL. Oh—like the railways?

BILLINGS (*dryly*) First service hot, second—cold.

POND. Oh, I was proposing the same menu for each.

BILLINGS (*looking meaningly at Pond*) So was I.

POND. Ha! I see your point. Well, I expect they'd like to lunch

at one, so as a matter of courtesy we might take the first service.
At twelve-thirty.

(BILLINGS *nods and indicates to Tassell to make a note of it.*
TASSELL *complies, making a "thumbs up" gesture with one thumb to
Billings*)

Next—classrooms. (*Grudgingly*) I'm afraid we shall have to allot
them some of those.

TASSELL. Unless, of course, they worked a night shift or something.

POND. There's no need to be flippant. I have the classrooms
worked out already. (*He sits* L *of the table* C) It involves a certain
amount of general post, but that's inevitable. (*He looks among his
papers and finds the relevant list*) I suggest as follows: (*He reads rapidly*)
"Upper Fourth combines with Lower Fifth. Lower Third to
Upper Fourth's room. Upper Fifth and Middle Fourth to Upper
Third. Fifth to Sixth, and vice versa." I think that's quite
straightforward.

BILLINGS. Oh, quite.

TASSELL (*a little dizzy*) What about Remove?

POND. Remove stays where it is. (*He indicates to Tassell that he
wants the notebook back*)

(TASSELL *passes the notebook to Pond*)

Thank you, Tassell. Oh, one other point. I'm afraid St Swithins
staff will have to use this common room. There's no alternative
to that.

BILLINGS (*rising and moving above the table* C) What about your
study?

TASSELL. Don't be silly—Mr Pond'll be sharing that with
Whitechapel.

BILLINGS. Of course—I hadn't thought of that. (*He moves up* L)

POND (*unhappily*) Neither had I.

(RAINBOW, *putting on his green baize apron, enters up* R, *leaving
the door open*)

RAINBOW (*to Pond*) Beg pardon, sir—the bus is just arriving.

POND (*absently*) Bring it in. (*He realizes*) Oh. (*He rises*) I mean
—there are two parcels of books on it, for me. Just put them in
my study. (*He moves above the table towards the doors up* R)

(TASSELL *rises, and he and* BILLINGS *move to the pegs* L *and put
on their mortar-boards and gowns*)

RAINBOW. Two parcels of books. In the study. Yes, sir.

(RAINBOW *exits up* R *leaving the* R *door open*)

POND (*hurriedly*) Billings—Tassell—see the boys in, will you?
(*He moves to the door up* R, *then pauses, having thought of something*) Oh,

and by-the-by, you'd better prepare them for the coming—ah—invasion. I shall, of course, address the school after roll-call, but in the meantime, you might just impress upon them that—er——

BILLINGS (*nodding*) Honoured guests.

TASSELL. No favouritism.

POND. Exactly. (*Briskly*) Now, I must go and talk to Mrs Hampstead about the stinks in the sinks—I mean—er—vice versa.

(POND *moves into the hall leaving the* R *door open, goes up the stairs and exits*)

TASSELL (*moving to the french windows*) I say, R.B., what are you going to say to your lot?

BILLINGS (*moving to the french windows and opening the* L *half of them*) I shall suggest that they give our honoured guests a very warm welcome.

(TASSELL *and* BILLINGS *exit by the french windows. An old-fashioned door-bell rings off. There is a pause, then the silence is broken by several imperative knocks on the front door. There is another pause and silence*)

WHITCHURCH (*off; calling*) Hullo. Someone.

(MISS EVELYN WHITCHURCH, *a formidable woman of about fifty, severely dressed in travelling clothes, enters by the french windows and sails across the stage to* R. *She is carrying an attaché case, a handbag and an umbrella.*

She is followed by MISS GOSSAGE, *who is hearty and bespectacled, with a red, scrubbed-looking face. She is in the middle thirties and wears tweeds with sensible shoes. She is carrying a kit-bag with a zip-fastener, and has a haversack slung across her shoulder*)

(*Looking around the room*) The Staff Common Room, I can only suppose. Huh! Encouraging. Outside—no answer. In here—no staff.

GOSSAGE (*standing up* L) Not very home from homey, is it?

WHITCHURCH (*putting the attaché case on the* R *end of the table* C) I've warned you, my dear Gossage, one cannot expect other schools to provide the comforts of St. Swithins.

GOSSAGE. Oh, I know, Miss Whitchurch. (*She moves* L *of the table* C) Still, I think they should make an effort. After all, atmosphere's jolly important. (*She puts her kit-bag down on the floor*)

WHITCHURCH. So is someone to answer the door. (*She moves to the doors up* R, *opens the* R *door, goes into the hall and calls up the stairs*) Hey there! Coo-ee! (*She calls again, exasperatedly*) Oh, coo-ee! (*She re-enters the room, leaving both doors open, and stands* R *of the table* C) The place is badly run, that's quite evident. We shall have to put a stop to that. Idle servants beget an idle staff. It spreads to the girls, and before you know where you are, your moral tone is in ribbons. (*She turns to the fireplace and runs her finger along the mantel-piece*) Look at that—inches thick.

GOSSAGE (*moving to the bookcase and running her finger along the ledge*) I say. You can write your name in it. (*She writes with her finger in the dust*) G-O-S-S . . .

WHITCHURCH (*moving above the R end of the table C*) Why bother. (*She looks at her brooch watch*) The girls will be here before we have even broken the ice. Did you watch our luggage on to the bus?

GOSSAGE (*turning from the bookcase*) Miss Harper took charge of it. (*She moves down L*) You wouldn't think any mistresses worth their salt would tolerate such a barracky old comm. (*She crosses to the fireplace*) Still, I expect we can soon jollify it up a bit.

WHITCHURCH. The room, possibly. Its occupants—I very much fear the worst. (*She puts her umbrella on the R end of the table C and surveys the clutter on the table*) Anyone content to live amid all this . . . (*She picks up the stick of rock*) Now I'm sure of the worst. Sucked at both ends.

GOSSAGE (*moving R of Miss Whitchurch*) What is it?

WHITCHURCH (*looking at the end of the piece of rock*) It says "Ilfracombe". Put it in the waste-paper basket. (*She hands the rock to Miss Gossage*) How nasty.

(MISS GOSSAGE *moves to the waste-paper basket and drops the piece of rock in it*)

(*She moves L of the table C, wipes her gloved fingers on her handkerchief, and notices the cricket bat*) Cricket, I see.

GOSSAGE (*moving below the table C, licking her sticky fingers*) Yes. You know, I'm afraid we shall have trouble with some of the girls. Netball in summer makes them absolutely melt.

WHITCHURCH. I thought that subject was closed, Miss Gossage. (*She starts to take off her gloves*) Melt or not, St Swithins has always played netball winter *and* summer. Cricket is no game for growing girls.

GOSSAGE. Most colls play it nowadays.

WHITCHURCH. If other schools choose to ruin their girls' figures, let them do so. (*She puts her gloves in her handbag*) Cricket thickens the biceps, enlarges the bust, and makes for very large hands and feet.

GOSSAGE. We don't really know that it does.

WHITCHURCH (*acidly*) Don't we? Look at these. (*She picks up Tassell's cricket boots*)

GOSSAGE. Perhaps you're right, Miss Whitchurch.

WHITCHURCH. Of course I'm right. (*She gives the boots to Miss Gossage*) Why, they're big enough for Don Bradshaw, or Brad-field, or whatever his name is.

(MISS GOSSAGE *takes the boots and puts them on the floor at the downstage end of the fender. As she does so, she sees the boxing-gloves on the easy chair by the fireplace*)

GOSSAGE (*staring at the gloves in amazement; in a puzzled tone*) Miss Whitchurch—— (*She picks up the gloves and holds them out for Miss Whitchurch to see*)

WHITCHURCH (*moving to Miss Gossage and taking the gloves gingerly; stunned*) Pugilism!

GOSSAGE. You don't suppose they teach it here?

WHITCHURCH (*moving below the table* c) Well, I don't suppose they wear them for walks. Of course, self-defence is invaluable to any girl—but of a lady-like kind—— (*She drops the left-hand boxing-glove on the table* c *and puts the other on her own right hand*)

GOSSAGE (*nodding*) After all, my ju-jitsu classes are equal to anything.

WHITCHURCH. Well, that explains the cricket, anyway. After a pummelling with these (*she hits her ungloved hand with the other*), I doubt if the girls have any figures left worth bothering about.

(RAINBOW, *carrying a parcel of books, enters up* R *and closes the* L *door. He is surprised at seeing the ladies and moves down* R *of Miss Whitchurch*)

(*Coldly*) Good afternoon.

RAINBOW. Good afternoon, madam.

WHITCHURCH. You are the school porter, I take it?

RAINBOW. Porter and groundsman.

WHITCHURCH. Name?

RAINBOW (*taken aback*) I beg your pardon?

WHITCHURCH. Your name? We might as well know it now as later.

RAINBOW (*looking at her curiously*) The name is Rainbow, madam.

WHITCHURCH (*after a moment*) Well, you can't help that. (*She gestures unthinkingly with the boxing-glove*)

(RAINBOW *ducks*)

I hope in future (*she removes the glove and puts it on the table* c) you will answer the door more promptly.

RAINBOW (*defensively*) I was out the front, madam, getting . . .

WHITCHURCH. That will do. *Qui s'excuse, s'accuse.*

RAINBOW. I beg your pardon?

WHITCHURCH. Granted—on this occasion. I want to see the Principal immediately.

RAINBOW. The Head, you mean?

WHITCHURCH. The Principal of Hilary Hall. As soon as possible.

RAINBOW (*crossing below Miss Whitchurch to the door down* L) The Head's busy just at the moment—with Matron. If you wouldn't mind waiting, madam——

WHITCHURCH. Just one moment.

(RAINBOW *pauses and turns*)

Before seeing the Principal, there is one thing I should like to know——

Rainbow. Yes, madam?

Whitchurch. How many mistresses have you?

Rainbow (*outraged*) I am a bachelor, madam, in every sense of the word.

(Rainbow *exits down* l., *closing the door behind him.* Miss Whitchurch *and* Miss Gossage *look after him curiously*)

Gossage (*moving above the* l *end of the table* c) What a rum sort of porter.

Whitchurch. Glandular trouble. (*She crosses to* r *of the table* c) The man is obviously at the awkward age.

Gossage. Seems a funny sort of school altogether. I wonder what the Principal's like?

Whitchurch (*picking up her umbrella*) I don't look forward at all to finding out. Anyone who could employ a man like that—— However, what can't be cured must be endured. I shall keep as aloof as possible. You, Miss Harper, and the girls will do the same.

Gossage. Yes, Miss Whitchurch.

(Rainbow *enters down* l *and crosses above the ladies to the doors up* r. *As he passes* Miss Whitchurch *she shudders. As* Rainbow *goes into the hall, he looks back at them, eyeing them curiously.* Miss Whitchurch *catches his eye and looks away hurriedly.*

Rainbow *exits down the passage* r, *leaving the* r *door open*)

Whitchurch. And I think the girls had better have an extra hour each week for ju-jitsu.

Gossage. Yes, Miss Whitchurch.

Whitchurch (*impatiently*) Well, I don't know how much longer this woman's going to be.

(Miss Gossage *moves outside the french windows and looks around*)

Perhaps we'd better reconnoitre on our own and take stock of the accommodation.

Gossage (*re-entering and moving above the table* c) It doesn't look a very large building for two schools.

Whitchurch. No. (*She moves to* r *of Miss Gossage*) We shall need quite three-quarters of it. I intend to let them know exactly how much we want—cut and dried, and no nonsense. One must be firm at the start, or . . .

(*She breaks off as* Rainbow, *carrying a second parcel of books, enters up* r. *He crosses to the door down* l *almost pushing between Miss Gossage and Miss Whitchurch*)

(*She protests*) Oh!

(Rainbow *turns, bumps the door open and exits*)

I suppose one can learn ju-jitsu at any age?

Gossage (*enthusiastically*) Oh yes, rather.

Whitchurch (*picking up her suitcase*) I may make it compulsory for the staff as well.

Gossage. Yes, Miss Whitchurch.

Whitchurch (*moving to the doors up* R) Come along, Gossage.

(Miss Gossage *picks up her kit-bag*)

Let's investigate this curious establishment. I doubt very much if it's even an approved school.

(Miss Whitchurch *and* Miss Gossage *exit down the passage* R *leaving both doors open.*

Rainbow *enters down* L, *looks surprised to find the room now empty, shrugs his shoulders and starts to cross to the door up* R.

As he does so, Pond *comes down the stairs and enters the room. He is carrying a book*)

Pond (*moving below the table* C) Did you bring them in?

Rainbow (L *of the table* C) No, sir. They come of their own accord.

Pond (*severely*) Don't be sarcastic, Rainbow, please. Where are they?

Rainbow. Gone of their own accord too, it seems. Daft, if you ask me, sir, the pair of them.

Pond (*exasperated*) What are you talking about, Rainbow? (*He crosses to the door down* L) Are those books in my study, or are they not?

Rainbow. The books are. The ladies aren't.

Pond (*turning*) What ladies?

Rainbow. There was two of them, sir, I think they was wanting. And they was wanting you, too, sir.

Pond. I'm expecting no-one. (*He turns again to the door down* L)

Rainbow (*with gloomy satisfaction*) Ah. Then perhaps that's why they've gone.

(Pond *nods and exits down* L. Rainbow *moves up* C.

As he does so, Billings *and* Tassell *enter from the passage up* R, *still wearing their mortar-boards and gowns. They leave the doors open*)

Billings (*seeing Rainbow*) So this is where you're skulking. Tuck-boxes. The bus driver refuses to bring them in single-handed. (*He crosses to the pegs* L, *takes off his mortar-board and gown, and hangs them up*)

Rainbow (*moving* R *of the table* C; *nodding gloomily*) They didn't ought to be allowed. Wicked, them things are. I strained my stomach once with a tuck-box.

Tassell (*moving* R *of Rainbow; grinning*) Funny—so did I.

Rainbow. Bound with iron at the corners.

TASSELL (*rubbing his stomach; ruefully*) That's just what it felt like.

RAINBOW (*moving to the doors up* R) And forty-six of 'em to bring in.

BILLINGS (*moving up* L; *cheerfully*) Not this afternoon. You'll have the St. Swithins ones, too. (*He notices the writing in the dust on the bookcase ledge, stops, and stares at it*)

RAINBOW. Murder, that's what it is.

(RAINBOW *exits up* R, *closing both doors behind him*)

TASSELL (*crossing to the pegs* L) Well, the little blighters look as healthy as always. (*He takes off his gown*)

BILLINGS (*staring at the writing in the dust*) What the devil's this?

TASSELL (*easing to the bookcase*) What's that?

BILLINGS. Something written in the dust—G-O-S—Gossage. (*He pronounces it as though it were French*)

TASSELL. What's Gossage?

BILLINGS (*moving to the chair* R *of the table* C) I don't know.

(TASSELL *moves to the pegs* L, *takes off his mortar-board and hangs it with his gown on the pegs*)

Must be some new rude word Rainbow picked up in the holidays. (*He sits*)

TASSELL (*moving below the table* C) How did your lot take the news? (*He perches himself on the table* C)

BILLINGS. About St Swithins?

(TASSELL *nods*)

With characteristic British phlegm.

TASSELL. Same here. Except for a certain amount of jubilation that it might mean one bath a week instead of two.

BILLINGS (*calmly*) I expect they'll be at each other's throats in the first five minutes.

TASSELL (*picking up the boxing-gloves with a grin and tying the laces together*) Better pass these on to Hopcroft Mi.—if his brother's left, I suppose they're his property now.

BILLINGS. If Hopcroft Mi. doesn't take to St Swithins, he won't be bothered by any Queensberry rules—something rude, swift, and below the belt is more in his line. That boy needs a firm hand —very firm—and this term he's going to get it.

(*There is a knock at the doors up* R)

Come in.

(HOPCROFT MI. *enters up* R, *closing the door behind him. He is a boy of about twelve, with a deceptively innocent air. He is dressed in a maroon-coloured blazer with yellow edgings, a grey shirt, Hilary Hall tie, grey shorts and stockings and black shoes*)

(*Fiercely*) Yes, Hopcroft, what is it?

HOPCROFT (*moving down* R *of Billings*) Please, sir, there's two strange ladies in the one downstairs.

BILLINGS (*rising and facing Hopcroft*) In the what?

HOPCROFT. The downstairs washroom, sir. There's two strange ladies in it.

(TASSELL *rises*)

BILLINGS. Hopcroft Minor, I don't want to chastise you on the first day of term——

TASSELL (*severely*) Vulgar without being funny. (*He moves up* LC)

HOPCROFT. But it's true, sir, honestly it is. There's a rummy looking one with spectacles on, and another rummy one without. And they've both got hats on.

BILLINGS. Fifty lines. By tomorrow evening.

HOPCROFT. But, sir——

(POND, *reading a letter he holds in his hand, enters down* L *and moves slowly below the table* C. *He has removed his mortar-board and gown*)

(*Hastily, as he sees Pond*) Yes, sir. What am I to write, sir?

BILLINGS (*turning to Pond*) "I must not be vulgar without being funny."

POND (*looking up*) I beg your pardon?

BILLINGS (*turning to Hopcroft; hurriedly*) I mean—Caesar—Gallic wars. First chapter.

HOPCROFT (*moving to the doors up* R) Yes, sir.

(BILLINGS *watches* HOPCROFT *as he exits, leaving the* R *door open.* TASSELL *moves above the chair* L *of the table* C)

POND. An imposition already?

BILLINGS (*turning to Pond*) You know what young Hopcroft is. It's an improvement on last term, anyway. I had to give him one then before we even left the station.

POND (*nodding*) A very difficult boy. (*He indicates the letter*) Oh —one of the new boys—Sowter, the name is—I've had a letter from his mother—she asks particularly that the boy should *not* be pampered.

TASSELL. That's a bit unusual, isn't it?

POND. Young Sowter has been at one of those advanced schools. Girls of all ages. Preparatory for boys.

BILLINGS. Sounds very advanced.

POND (*looking at Billings*) Possibly. Yet the boy is backward in his work——

TASSELL (*moving down* L) I'm not surprised.

POND (*moving* R *of Tassell*) The parents look to us to eradicate any traces of feminine influence.

BILLINGS (*moving* R *of Pond*) Leave him to me.

TASSELL (*with feeling*) I shouldn't worry. He'll have to look a long way for feminine influence in this part of the world.

POND (*approvingly*) Quite. I was happy to write and assure Mrs Sowter that the teaching staff here is entirely male—and bachelors into the bargain. I quoted her the school motto— "Homo in Omnibus"—"A Man In All Things".

TASSELL (*pleased to be enlightened*) So that's what it means. I always used to think it was something to do with strap-hanging.

(*Before Pond can comment on this,* BARBARA CAHOUN *enters up* R. *She is a self-confident, hearty girl of fourteen, dressed in the St Swithins school outfit. She is carrying a tennis racquet, a camera case, a suitcase, a mackintosh and the jacket of Miss Harper's costume*)

BARBARA. I say, excuse me . . .

(POND, BILLINGS *and* TASSELL *all turn* R *together, startled*)

Do you know—is this the Staff Common Room?

POND. It is.

BARBARA (*moving above the* R *end of the table* C) Thanks awfully. (*Enthusiastically*) Miss Harper let me carry her things in from the bus.

BILLINGS. Miss Harper? (*He moves to the table* C *and pulls out the chair* L *of it*)

BARBARA. Yes—she's awfully decent like that. Well—in fact, she's really absolutely top score altogether, actually. (*She looks around for somewhere to put her load—and sweeps Billings' and Tassell's things off the table* C)

(BILLINGS *catches as many as he can, collapsing into the chair* L *of the table as he does so.* BARBARA *carefully puts Miss Harper's belongings on the table, stroking the mackintosh as she lays it down.* POND *and* TASSELL *look at her in amazement. She beams at them, then moves to the doors up* R)

POND (*suddenly jerking out of his astonishment*) Here—girl—young lady—just a moment, please.

(BILLINGS *rises and dumps the articles he is holding into the easy chair up* L)

BARBARA (*turning*) I can't stop more than a sec. (*She moves down* R *of the table* C) If I'm caught jawing in here I'll be given a miss.

BILLINGS (*moving between Pond and Tassell*) Given a miss?

BARBARA (*patiently*) Misconduct mark. They're awfully strict at St Swithins. You get one for practically anything.

TASSELL ⎫
POND ⎬ (*each taking a step forward; together*) Did you say St
BILLINGS ⎭ Swithins?

BARBARA (*nodding*) Yes. I suppose you're Hilary Hall. They don't let parents come down on our first day.

BILLINGS. Parents . . .

TASSELL. We're not . . .

BARBARA. Rotten, isn't it? I say, I must fly, really—— (*She runs to the doors up* R)

POND (*firmly*) Wait, please.

(BARBARA *stops and turns*)

Are we to understand that you are a pupil at St Swithins?

BARBARA (*moving* R *of the table, nodding*) I'm in the Lower Fifth. Barbara Cahoun. *Not* spelt Colquhoun.

BILLINGS (*disgustedly*) Do you mean to say they have girls at St Swithins?

BARBARA (*giggling*) Well, I should hope so—it's a girls' school.

(POND *collapses into* BILLINGS' *arms.* TASSELL *helps to support* BILLINGS)

TASSELL⎱ (*together; staggered*) ⎰It's what?
POND ⎰   ⎱It can't be.

BILLINGS. Of course it can't. (*He eyes Barbara dryly*) This is a female Hopcroft of some sort. (*Crossing below Pond to Barbara*) Can you truthfully stand there and tell us that St Swithins, Hastings, is a girls' school?

BARBARA. No. St Leonards.

BILLINGS (*turning triumphantly to Pond*) There you are.

TASSELL. You said St Swithins just now.

BARBARA. St Swithins, St Leonards. St Swithins, Hastings is boys. We're St Swithins, St Leonards. And we're girls, see? Och, it's quite easy, really. So long.

(BARBARA *skips up* R *and exits, closing the doors behind her.* POND, BILLINGS *and* TASSELL *look after her in utter consternation*)

POND (*aghast*) You don't suppose she's telling the truth?

BILLINGS (*moving round* R *of the table* C *to the bookcase*) We can easily find out—there's a schools directory in here somewhere—— (*He searches in the bookcase*)

(TASSELL *moves* C *above the table* C)

POND (*moving* L *of the table* C) The wire came from Hastings—of that I'm positive. (*He looks at the telegram*)

BILLINGS (*locating the directory*) Here we are. (*He turns and puts the book on the table* C)

(POND *looks over* BILLINGS' *left shoulder.* TASSELL *over* BILLINGS' *right*)

(*He turns the pages and reads*) "St Leonards—see Hastings and St Leonards." (*To Pond*) They're both under the same heading.

TASSELL. That explains the wire.

BILLINGS (*moving his finger down the page*) S—S—here we are——
(*He reads*) "St Alfred's, St Arthur's, St Bride's"——

POND (*impatiently*) S—you want.

BILLINGS. I'm looking under S.

TASSELL. Saint S, he means. S—S.

BILLINGS. Don't hiss at me—here we are—— (*He reads*) "St
Swithins—Boys—Boarding."

POND. Boys. There. That's the one in the wire, of course.

BILLINGS (*reading*) "Headmaster, O. J. Philpott." (*He looks at
the telegram in Pond's hand*) And that *isn't* the one in the wire.

TASSELL. No. That was old Whitechapel.

BILLINGS (*reading on*) "St Swithins—Girls—Boarding. Principal, Miss Evelyn Whitchurch, M.A. Oxon." (*He looks at the
telegram again. Grimly*) Well, that seems to settle it. (*He closes the
directory*)

POND (*staring at the directory*) But it's impossible. We can't have
a girls' school here.

BILLINGS. You've got one.

TASSELL. The Ministry must have put its foot in it.

BILLINGS (*crossing above Tassell to the fireplace*) And their yea is
yea and their nay is nay.

POND (*agitatedly*) We must do something post-haste—contact
the Ministry before they arrive.

BILLINGS (*pacing up* R) They *have* arrived. (*He turns*)

(TASSELL *moves up* L)

You saw that Cahoun thing—not spelt Colquhoun. (*He paces
down* R)

(TASSELL *paces down* L *in unison with* BILLINGS)

And that's only a sample. There'll be girls and mistresses all over
the place.

(BILLINGS *and* TASSELL *continue to pace in unison up and down*
R *and* L *respectively*)

TASSELL. Committing misconduct marks in all directions.

BILLINGS. We'll be engulfed in hockey and cocoa.

POND (*groaning*) Great Heaven forbid. (*He suddenly remembers
and bangs the table* C) The wanting women.

BILLINGS. The what?

POND. Two of them—and Rainbow said they were looking
for me.

BILLINGS (*at the fireplace*) One with spectacles and one without?

TASSELL (L *of the table* C) And they've both got hats on?

POND. Heaven knows. But if one's that Whitchurch woman—
and she's at large—goodness knows what she might be up to.
(*He hurries to the doors up* R) She may be anywhere.

(POND *exits up* R, *leaving the* L *door open*. BILLINGS *hurries up* R *after him*)

BILLINGS (*calling*) Try the one downstairs. (*He closes the door, moves to the table* C, *collects the directory and puts it on the bookcase ledge*) Well, this is a nice thing, I must say. (*He moves to the fireplace*)

TASSELL (*grinning*) So must I. (*He moves below the table* C *to* R *of it*) The more I think about it, the nicer it seems. Here was I moaning about the lack of feminine society, and what happens? (*He sits in the chair* R *of the table* C) St Swithins from sunny St Leonards-on-Sea.

BILLINGS (*coldly*) I'm surprised at you. (*He crosses below the table* C)

TASSELL. What do you mean?

BILLINGS (*turning*) If your idea of feminine society ranges from seven years to fourteen——

TASSELL. Don't be a chump. It's mistresses I'm thinking of. (*He adds quickly*) Schoolmistresses.

BILLINGS (*perching himself on the table* C) Have you ever met any?

TASSELL (*thinking*) No. I don't think I have.

BILLINGS. I thought not. They fall into two groups——

TASSELL. All of them?

BILLINGS. All of them. Group one—The Battle-axe—baleful, brainy and belligerent. Group two—The Hearty Amazon—healthy, High School and hail-fellow-well-met. (*He goes through the motions of slapping Tassell on the back*)

TASSELL. Damn it, there must be some attractive ones.

BILLINGS. None.

TASSELL. What will you bet me?

BILLINGS (*rising and moving* L *of the table* C) Anything you like. I can't lose. How much do you want on the St Swithins lot—five pounds?

TASSELL (*dubiously*) Well—five bob.

BILLINGS. Done. (*While he continues speaking, he picks up Miss Harper's belongings from the table* C *and dumps them on the chair above the door* L. *He then returns his own and Tassell's property from the floor and the easy chair up* L) And I may say right from the start, there's going to be no women and children first nonsense, where I'm concerned—male or female, they will all come in the honoured guests category, and will be treated as such. (*He moves down* L)

TASSELL (*rising and moving to* R *of Billings*) You go your way, I go mine. Personally, I shall extend to the St Swithins staff the outstretched hand of welcome. (*He gestures appropriately to the doors up* R)

(*As he does so, the doors up* R *are opened and* POND *ushers in* MISS WHITCHURCH *and* MISS GOSSAGE. TASSELL *looks considerably taken aback by their appearance as they stare icily. Both ladies have taken off their hats and coats.* MISS GOSSAGE *moves below the fireplace,* MISS WHITCHURCH *slightly above her, and* POND *to R of the table* C)

POND (*to Miss Whitchurch*) Allow me to present my staff. Mr Tassell—Science, English and Mathematics. Mr Billings—Modern Languages, History and Geography.

(BILLINGS *and* TASSELL *incline their heads politely*)

(*To Billings and* TASSELL) This is Miss Whitchurch, M.A.
BILLINGS (*into Tassell's left ear; quietly*) Oxon.
POND. Headmistress of St Swithins.
WHITCHURCH (*correcting him, severely*) Principal.
POND. I beg your pardon.
BILLINGS (*to Tassell*) Group one.

(POND *reacts slightly*)

POND. And this is Miss Gossage . . .
BILLINGS⎱ (*together, to each other, pronouncing it as though it were*
TASSELL ⎰   *French*) Gossage!
GOSSAGE (*beaming*) Games, Maths, Botany, Drawing, Needlework, Handicraft, and Extras. (*She energetically crosses L and wrings their hands painfully, first Tassell, then Billings at whom she stands beaming*)
TASSELL (*nursing the hand that has been shaken; to Billings, weakly*) Group two?

(BILLINGS *nods triumphantly.* TASSELL *resignedly takes two half-crowns from his pocket, and with* MISS GOSSAGE *standing between him and Billings, beaming from one to the other, manages to pass over the money without her seeing it*)

POND (*clearing his throat; severely*) This, of course, is our Common Staff—er—Staff Common Room.

(MISS GOSSAGE *moves to the french windows*)

WHITCHURCH. Quite. I hope we shan't have to put up with it for long.

(POND *looks askance*)

The position is quite impossible. Sharing premises at all is distasteful enough—but with a boys' school . . . (*She crosses Pond and sits in the chair R of the table* C) The matter must be rectified at once.
POND. I entirely agree.
BILLINGS (*crossing Tassell to L of the table* C; *helpfully*) There's a very good train back at five-twenty.
WHITCHURCH (*with a wintry smile*) It's hardly a matter of trains, I'm afraid. We shall have to find somewhere else to go.
POND. There's nowhere at St Leonards? (*He eases to the fireplace and stands with his back to it*)

WHITCHURCH (*amused*) St Leonards? (*She laughs mirthlessly*) D'you hear that, Miss Gossage?

(MISS GOSSAGE *echoes the mirthless laugh, and moves above the table* C)

(*To Pond*) St Swithins has not been at St Leonards for five years. It'll be another year at least before we can go back. I went to see the building yesterday. It wasn't there. Flat. Quite flat.

GOSSAGE (*standing behind Miss Whitchurch's chair, explaining*) We were evacuated to St Philippa's at St Anne's, with St Hilda's and St Matilda's.

BILLINGS. Well, couldn't you go back there—from St Pancras?

WHITCHURCH. No room. St Philippa's had to have their buildings back. You see *they'd* been evacuated to St Mary's at St Ives, St Mary's having gone to All Saints at Oxford. I don't know where All Saints went to.

BILLINGS (*turning to Tassell; quietly*) I've got a rough idea.

(JOYCE HARPER *enters up* R, *closing the door behind her. She is a very attractive girl in the early twenties*)

JOYCE (*moving* R *of Miss Whitchurch; with some concern*) Miss Whitchurch——

WHITCHURCH. Ah, Miss Harper——

JOYCE. I think there must be something wrong—there's a crowd of small boys about the place, all staring with their mouths open and not saying a word——

WHITCHURCH. There's been a slight misunderstanding at the Ministry. This is Mr Pond, Principal of Hilary Hall.

POND (*retaliating*) Headmaster. (*He shakes hands with Joyce*)

JOYCE (*understanding now*) It's a boys' school.

WHITCHURCH. Exactly. Where did you leave the girls?

JOYCE. They went upstairs with Matron.

WHITCHURCH (*aghast*) *Their* matron?

BILLINGS (*with mild sarcasm*) It's all right, she's a woman.

TASSELL (*twirling an imaginary moustache*) You might not think so, but she is.

(MISS WHITCHURCH *glares at Tassell, then waves a hand in introduction*)

WHITCHURCH (*to Joyce; in a tone of some disparagement*) These are the remains of their staff. Mr—er——

BILLINGS (*dryly*) Billings.

WHITCHURCH. Billings.

JOYCE (*crossing below the table* C *to Billings*) How do you do? (*Her eyes are on Tassell*)

BILLINGS (*offhandedly*) How do you do? (*He shakes hands with her*)

TASSELL (*pulling Billings out of the way, and taking Joyce's hand*) Tassell. (*He shakes hands with her warmly*)

JOYCE (*smiling*) How d'you do?

TASSELL. Oh, fine now, thanks. (*A little anxiously*) You really are on the staff of St Swithins?

JOYCE (*smiling*) Yes. Why not?

TASSELL. No reason at all. Absolutely none. (*He laughs*)

(JOYCE *tries to withdraw her hand*)

(*He realizes he is still holding her hand*) Oh! (*He releases it and turns to Billings*) Group three, I think.

(BILLINGS *resignedly takes a ten-shilling note from his pocket and pays it to Tassell.* MISS WHITCHURCH *and* MISS GOSSAGE *look increasingly surprised.* POND *coughs*)

(*He sees them staring*) Just a small bet we had.

WHITCHURCH (*acidly*) Horses?

BILLINGS (*dryly*) The losers were.

WHITCHURCH (*severely*) As I was saying, the sooner we can find other quarters, the better. (*To Pond*) I shall telephone the Ministry at once. (*She rises*) I suppose you are on the telephone out here?

(MISS GOSSAGE *moves above the table* C. JOYCE *moves to the french windows*)

POND (*with umbrage*) We are. In several places. Here, Matron's room, my study——

WHITCHURCH. Kindly conduct me to your study.

POND (*crossing below the table to the door down* L) This way.

(MISS WHITCHURCH *follows him.* TASSELL *and* BILLINGS, *who are standing* LC *side by side, take a simultaneous step backwards up stage as she passes them.*

    POND *and* MISS WHITCHURCH *exit down* L. JOYCE *looks around for her belongings*)

JOYCE (*moving above the table* C) Did someone bring my things in?

(MISS GOSSAGE *points to them on the chair* L, *moves to the french windows and gazes out*)

TASSELL. Your things? Oh, rather—yes. We put them here, out of the way, for safety. (*He picks up Joyce's property from the chair, takes them to the table* C, *sweeps Billings' belongings off the table again into Billings' hands, and puts Joyce's things carefully on the table, stroking the mackintosh in the same way that Barbara did*)

(BILLINGS, *who has sprung to catch his property, continues the movement until he pulls up near the french windows*)

JOYCE (R *of Tassel*) Thank you so much.

BILLINGS. Yes—thank you *so* much.

Joyce. I suppose we shall be here for a day or two anyway.
Tassell. Oh, yes—several days or two, I hope.
Joyce (*picking up her suitcase*) I think I'll take this upstairs.
Tassell (*eagerly*) You can't possibly manage it. (*He takes the suitcase from her*) Let me carry it for you.

(Joyce *and* Tassell *move to the door up* r)

Gossage (*turning*) We don't know yet where our bedrooms will be.
Billings (*easing down* lc) Second corridor on the left, far end.
Tassell. Don't be silly, old boy, that's the carpenter's shop. (*To Joyce*) You're going to sleep in my room.
Billings. What?

(Joyce *reacts*)

Tassell. I mean—well, come with me and I'll show you what I mean.

(Joyce *reacts again*)
      Tassell *hastily opens the door and they exit, closing the door behind them.* Billings *moves below the table* c)

Gossage (*moving down* l) I say, Mr Billings, I don't think much of your stuffy old comm.
Billings (*surprised*) My what? (*He looks hurriedly at the things he is holding*) It isn't—it's a scarf.
Gossage. The common room, I mean. We had a really topping den at St Swithins. But then, of course, men on their own are so helpless. (*She looks at the scarf*) Are those the Hilary Hall colours?
Billings. Blood and orange.
Gossage. Ours are pale blue and puce.
Billings (*disgusted*) Spiffing. (*He piles his property back on to the table* c)
Gossage. They are, rather. (*She steps nearer to Billings. A little coyly*) Of course, crimson is more my colour really.
Billings. Oh, I wouldn't say that.
Gossage (*picking up the cricket bat*) It's a pity we won't be staying—I hoped we might convert Miss Whitchurch to cricket. I've been trying for years, you know.
Billings. A bit old for it, isn't she?
Gossage. For the girls, I mean. Of course she's thinking of their figures, but I was an absolute demon for it. (*She tries a sweeping stroke with the bat*)

(Billings *dodges and tries to grab the end of the bat*)

I can't see what she's afraid of, can you? (*She makes another wild stroke, nearly hitting Billings*)
Billings (*retreating to the fireplace*) No—but I can imagine.

Gossage. My pater always said he thought I'd shape very well. (*She takes up a cricket stance, facing the audience*)

Billings. We all make mistakes.

Gossage. I'm so glad you agree. (*She runs across to Billings and hands him the bat*) Perhaps before we go, I can try my hand out on the pitch. (*She turns and paces out a bowler's run down stage L where she makes a mark in the carpet with the side of her foot*) I used to be quite a wizard at yorkers. (*She faces Billings and shouts*) Play. (*She runs to the fireplace, swinging her right arm over as if bowling, her run finishing by her cannoning into the fire-irons*)

(Billings *dodges down* R)

But there, I expect you'd hit me for six. (*She bends over to straighten the fire-irons*)

Billings (*with feeling*) I'd have a good try. (*He sees her bending, and swinging the bat, can scarcely refrain from hitting her*)

(Miss Whitchurch, *followed by* Pond, *enters down* L. Miss Gossage *straightens up and turns*)

Gossage (*moving above the* L *end of the table* C) Mr Billings was just saying, Miss Whitchurch, that he thinks cricket would be a ripping thing for the girls.

Billings (*moving above the stool down* R) What I really meant was . . . (*He hits the stool with the bat, which he then stands in the corner behind the telephone table*)

Pond (*crossing to the fireplace; crushingly*) Never mind that now, Billings, please. We've got other things to think of. (*He corrects himself in vexation*) Of which to think. All this is playing havoc with my grammar.

(Rainbow, *now wearing a white apron, opens the doors up* R, *picks up the school bell from the window-sill, and starts to ring the bell furiously*)

(*Distractedly*) Oh, my goodness. (*He moves to the doors up* R *and closes them to muffle the sound*)

(Miss Whitchurch *puts her fingers to her ears*)

Gossage (*moving above Miss Whitchurch to* L *of her; shouting*) What did the Ministry say, Miss Whitchurch?

(*The bell stops*)

(*To Miss Whitchurch, still shouting*) It's stopped. It's stopped.

Whitchurch (*taking her fingers from her ears*) There's no need to shout.

Gossage. What did the Ministry say?

Whitchurch (*heatedly*) They won't even admit their mistake. They say I must be a boys' school—I'm on a blue card in the index.

(Miss Gossage *eases down* l. Pond *eases* r *of the table* c)

I spoke to three different grades of civil servant, telling them to change my colour immediately. They all refused. One of them had the impertinence to say he had no evidence as to my sex over the telephone.

Gossage (*moving in* l *of Miss Whitchurch*) One really wants a chin-wag with the man at the top.

(Billings *looks at Miss Gossage, pained*)

Whitchurch (*annoyed*) The Controller is down with flu, the Sub-Controller is sitting on a Standing Committee, and the Deputy Sub-Controller, Mr Fraphampton, has gone to a kindergarten in Wales.

Billings. About time too, I should think.

Whitchurch (*moving to the chair* r *of the table* c) He'll be there till next Monday. (*She sits*) Until then, nothing at all can be done.

Pond (*nodding*) Just for a week we shall have to accept the present state of affairs.

(Miss Gossage *moves* l *of the table* c)

(*To Miss Whitchurch*) Now, about accommodation—we haven't much to offer, I'm afraid——

Whitchurch (*briskly*) We shall cheerfully put up with the best you have.

(Miss Gossage *moves to the french windows and turns*)

Pond (*swallowing*) Oh, thank you. Well now, I've made out a tentative list—— (*He takes a small sheet of paper from his pocket*)

Whitchurch. I've made out a definite one. (*She rises and produces a large sheet of foolscap from her pocket*) These are our exact requirements—no more, no less. (*She hands the list to Pond*)

Pond (*looking at the list unhappily*) Oh.

Whitchurch. It's quite clear, I hope?

Pond. Oh, quite. (*He puts the list in his pocket*)

Whitchurch. May I see yours?

Pond (*hastily*) I—ah—don't think I should bother. (*He looks helplessly at Billings*) A little too tentative. (*He tears up his own list*)

(Billings *picks up the waste-paper basket and holds it out to* Pond, *who drops the remains of his list in it.* Billings *replaces the basket on the floor.*

Tassell *and* Joyce, *now without her hat and gloves, enter up* r. Joyce *moves above the* l *end of the table* c)

Tassell (*as they enter*) What's the news from the Ministry? (*He moves to* l *of Pond*)

Pond. Most disappointing.

B

TASSELL (*turning to Miss Whitchurch; dismayed*) You're going?

WHITCHURCH. On the contrary. We have to stay for a week at least.

TASSELL (*delighted*) A week. (*He moves above the table to* L *of Joyce*) Oh, I say, that's terrible, isn't it?

(BILLINGS *eyes Tassell dryly*)

GOSSAGE (*moving down* L; *suddenly*) Jiminy!

POND. I beg your pardon?

GOSSAGE. What about the parents?

WHITCHURCH (*moving below the table* C) *What* about the parents?

GOSSAGE. If I know anything of ours, they'll kick up an awful fuss when they find out.

BILLINGS. Ours will raise the devil.

POND. Hm—yes—I hadn't thought of that.

(RAINBOW *enters up* R. *He looks a little worried*)

RAINBOW (*in the doorway*) Beg pardon, sir——

POND (*abstractedly*) In a few minutes, Rainbow, please.

RAINBOW. Yes, sir.

(RAINBOW *exits up* R *closing the doors*)

POND (*moving* R *of Miss Whitchurch*) Parents, yes—there's a pretty problem in that direction.

JOYCE (*moving below the* L *end of the table* C) But it's nobody's fault—it's the Ministry's.

WHITCHURCH. Do you seriously think, Miss Harper, that parents are going to blame the Ministry? Parents *always* blame the school.

POND. Quite right.

WHITCHURCH (*indignantly*) What d'you mean—quite right?

POND. I'm not approving, I'm agreeing. Quite right.

TASSELL. The thing is—need they find out?

GOSSAGE. Letters home.

TASSELL. Not in the first week, surely?

WHITCHURCH. Every girl writes home twice a week regularly, Wednesdays and Saturdays.

JOYCE. And the first evening—to say they've arrived safely.

POND. There's only one way out. We must appeal to their sense of public duty——

(TASSELL *crosses above the table* C *to* L *of Billings*)

—apart, of course, from censoring the correspondence.

WHITCHURCH. I shall do the same. It's the only way to prevent a leakage.

BILLINGS (*sarcastically*) Short of locking 'em all up and dictating a circular letter.

POND. Oh, I hardly think we need go as far as that.

(Rainbow *enters up* R, *looking rather more worried than before. He closes the doors behind him*)

Rainbow (*to Pond*) Beg pardon, sir——
Pond (*exasperatedly*) I asked you to wait, Rainbow.

(Rainbow *waits up* R, *but indicates to Tassell that there is something wrong in the school*)

Gossage (*crossing Joyce to* L *of Miss Whitchurch*) It's going to be a full-time job, steaming all their letters open.
Whitchurch (*shocked*) Miss Gossage, you don't seriously suggest that St Swithins should stoop to steaming?
Gossage (*moving* L *of the table* c) Well, I don't see how else it can be done.
Whitchurch. The girls will be told to leave their envelopes unstuck—on hygienic grounds.
Pond. Personally, I prefer to be quite open about it. I shall tell the boys we intend to check their spelling.
Billings. What could be more open than that?

(Rainbow, *unable to control his agitation any longer, moves above Tassell and Billings to the telephone on the table down* R, *lifts the receiver and dials a number*)

Pond. Well, I'm sure we shall all try to make the best of things —boys and girls, masters and mistresses.
Whitchurch. Hear, hear.
Tassell (*looking at Joyce*) We certainly will, won't we, Miss Harper?
Gossage. It may be rather a sticky wicket, but we'll toe the line and turn up trumps, won't we, Mr Billings? (*She beams at Billings*)

(Billings *winces*)

Pond (*to Miss Whitchurch*) Suppose we shake on that? (*He holds out his hand*) On behalf of Hilary Hall.
Whitchurch (*shaking hands with Pond; with dignity*) Floreat St Swithins.
Gossage (*slapping Joyce on the back*) Floreat St Swithins. (*She shakes hands with Joyce*)
Billings (*shaking hands, mock-heroically, with Tassell*) Homo in Omnibus.
Rainbow (*speaking into the telephone*) Hullo . . .

(*The hand-shaking stops*)

Is that Dr Hodges . . .

(*They all turn and look at Rainbow*)

I'm speaking from the school . . .

POND (*sharply*) Dr Hodges——?

RAINBOW (*speaking into the telephone*) Yes . . . I'm afraid we're going to have some casualities.

WHITCHURCH (*aghast*) "Casualities"?

RAINBOW (*speaking into the telephone*) Yes . . . Some of the pupils . . .

(*They all close in on Rainbow*)

POND (*angrily*) Rainbow—explain yourself.

RAINBOW (*speaking into the telephone*) Just a minute, Doctor. (*He turns to Pond*) I rung the tea bell. The young ladies come in first. The young gentlemen didn't take very kindly to tnat. They're in the dining hall now—both lots.

GOSSAGE. Eating?

RAINBOW. Eating each other, if you ask me.

(*Children's voices are heard off, raised in altercation*)

There was only words at first, but after the first fishcakes was thrown——

WHITCHURCH. They're throwing fishcakes?

RAINBOW (*with gloomy satisfaction*) And the sauce along with 'em.

(*There is a crash of crockery and louder children's voices off*)

(*With more gloomy satisfaction*) They're getting warmed up now.

POND. Oh, my goodness!

WHITCHURCH (*in anguish*) My girls.

GOSSAGE (*hurrying to the doors up* R: *frantically*) Which way?

TASSELL (*hurrying to the doors up* R) Follow me.

(*Led by* TASSELL, *all except* RAINBOW *and* BILLINGS *rush for the doors up* R. *As they scramble for precedence in the doorway,* BARBARA, *now without her hat and blazer, comes down the stairs, with an envelope in her hand*)

BARBARA (*fighting her way through the scramble into the room*) Please, where's the post-box?

(*They sweep past her and exit down the passage to* R. *As* BARBARA *looks round bewildered,* POND *re-enters quickly and snatches the envelope out of her hand*)

POND. No good—censored.

(*POND exits hurriedly down the passage to* R)

BARBARA (*running after him; calling indignantly*) Hey!

(*BARBARA exits at a run down the passage to* R.

BILLINGS *watches all this with sardonic enjoyment. When they have all gone, he moves to the doors up* R *and closes them. There is a moment's quiet as he moves to the table* C *and starts to fold his scarf*)

RAINBOW (*speaking into the telephone*) Are you still there, Doctor? . . . I'm sorry about that . . . I think there'll be one or two adults in addition . . . (*He replaces the receiver and starts to move to the doors up* R)

BILLINGS. Er—Rainbow . . .

(RAINBOW *pauses*)

You didn't happen to see who threw the first fishcake?

RAINBOW. Hopcroft Minor.

BILLINGS (*grinning*) Ah. You might give him a message for me.

RAINBOW. A message, sir?

BILLINGS (*moving to his locker, carrying his scarf*) Tell him I've cancelled those fifty lines.

RAINBOW *exits up* R *as—*

the CURTAIN *falls*

ACT II

SCENE—*The same. Saturday afternoon, three weeks later.*

Under Miss Gossage's influence, the Common Room has been duly jollified. There is a warm-coloured table-cloth on the refectory table, which is now set up and down stage, slightly R. The three small chairs are still L, R, and above it. The dining chair from above the study door is now standing LC facing the audience, and its place has been taken by the easy chair from up L. Both easy chairs and the window seats now have bright cushions. The brown rug by the fireplace has been replaced by a brighter one, and there are bright rugs in the hall, in front of the door down L, and on the floor L of the table C. Net curtains hang at the sides of the french windows. The figures from the mantelpiece have been transferred and stand, one each on top of the lockers R. The mantelpiece is furnished with an Ormulu clock, two Japanese china vases, and two other tall vases. In the fire-grate stands a brown jug filled with beech-leaves. Three small silver cups have been added to those already on the top of the bookcase. The respective groups are clearly labelled "St Swithins" and "Hilary Hall". The map over the door down L has been replaced by a bright poster picture. The notice board in the hall has been divided vertically by a white tape, one half headed "Hilary Hall" and the other "St Swithins". Three brightly coloured magazines for women have replaced the old ones on the table down R. The mortar-boards and gowns have gone from the pegs L. A cricket bat stands in the corner above the fireplace.

When the CURTAIN rises JOYCE is seated in the armchair L, marking a pile of well-thumbed exercise-books with a pencil. MISS GOSSAGE is seated in the chair LC with a mark-book and pencil, going through some fancy needlework. A round shallow work-basket on the floor R of her chair contains a pair of gaily patterned feminine pyjamas with a frill on the bottom of each leg, a pair of very diaphanous knickers, a night-dress with smocking on it, and various other pieces of needlework. BILLINGS and TASSELL, both censoring letters, are seated L and R respectively of the table C on which is a blue vase filled with sprays of wild flowers and grasses, two piles of stamped and addressed envelopes, a number still unsealed, and a piece of india-rubber. Both the french windows are open. The double doors are closed.

TASSELL. This is an easy job. The little blighters write the same letter home every week. The only thing that changes is the date.

JOYCE (*smiling*) And the excuses for more pocket money.

BILLINGS. Well, I'm damned. That's the fourth time that boy has put "To Hell with St Swithins" after his signature.

TASSELL. He must be a sort of one-man resistance movement.

JOYCE. How do you cope with it?

32

BILLINGS. Blot it out. (*He shakes some ink from his pen on to the letter*) After all, what's one blot more among so many? (*He holds up a much-blotted letter*)

TASSELL. Talk about tact—listen to this one from young Sowter. (*He reads*) "Dear Mother and Father, This is a very nice school. Mr Pond, the headmastei, is very nice. So is Mr Billings. Mr Tassell is very nice too. No more news now. Your loving son, Cyril. P.S. Matron is also very nice."

(TASSELL *laughs across to* JOYCE *who laughs back*)

BILLINGS (*to Tassell; disgustedly*) Get on with it.

GOSSAGE (*looking at the frilly pair of pyjamas*) The Lower Third's fancy work is coming along like Billy-o. (*She makes an entry in the mark-book*) I'm giving Penelope Bagshott an alpha plus this week. (*She holds up the pyjamas*) Look at these pyjees, aren't they absolutely tiptop? (*She leans across and taps Billings on the shoulder*)

BILLINGS (*turning; dryly*) Corking.

GOSSAGE. The best little needlewoman in the whole lower school. (*She suddenly notices something about the garment*) Oh dear— she's made a fearful hash of her scallops. It'll have to be a minus after all. Where's my bungy? (*She rises and moves above Billings to the table* c)

BILLINGS (*wincing; and copying her voice*) Where's her bungy? (*As he turns to look up stage at her, he gets his face in the flowers*)

GOSSAGE (*brightly*) We picked those this morning—on our nature study ramble.

BILLINGS. Next time I should go where the grass is shorter. (*He rises, picks up the vase and moves as though to take it out of the french windows*)

GOSSAGE (*moving to stop him, dismayed*) Oh—you're not going to move them? It's Old Man's Beard and Queen Anne's Lace.

BILLINGS (*crossing to the waste-paper basket down* R) The old Man's Beard is withered and Queen Anne's Lace is dead. (*He takes the flowers from the vase*) If you don't mind, therefore, I shall deposit them in the wagger-pagger-bagger. (*He drops the flowers into the waste-paper basket*)

GOSSAGE (*picking up the india-rubber, moving to her chair* LC *and sitting; reproachfully*) You *are* a bear with a sore head. Must have got out of bed the wrong side. (*She corrects the entry in her mark-book, then resumes examining the needlework*)

TASSELL (*taking his cigarette-case from his pocket*) He did. Sore head was the result. He hit it on a vice.

BILLINGS (*moving to his chair* L *of the table* C; *bitterly*) As a bedroom, the carpenter's shop has its disadvantages.

TASSELL. All the same, I don't know why you got out that side.

BILLINGS (*acidly*) Because on the other, I trod on a chisel. A St Swithins chisel at that. (*To Joyce*) I've spoken about it.

(TASSELL *offers Billings a cigarette, and takes one himself*)

(*He takes a cigarette*) Thanks. (*He sits*) Reminds me, I must get some New-skin from Mrs Hampstead. (*He feels his heel tenderly*)

GOSSAGE (*looking at the pair of knickers and shaking her head*) Her gussets are miles too large.

BILLINGS (*with umbrage*) Mrs Hampstead's gussets are entirely a Hilary Hall affair. (*He leans back in his chair and during Miss Gossage's next speech makes appropriate but insincere reactions*)

GOSSAGE (*marking her book; sweetly*) These aren't Mrs Hampstead's—they're Audrey Thomson's. Poor child. All thumbs. Quite apart from her gussets, she simply will not neaten her necklines properly, her smocking is shocking, and last week she had to untack every one of her tucks.

(BILLINGS *turns back to the table and buries his head in his hands*)

(*She looks at her wrist-watch*) By Jove, it's getting on for netters time—I must dash up and change. (*She rises, dumps the work-basket, mark-book, etc. on the downstage end of the table* C, *moves to the doors up* R, *opens the* L *door, turns, and, offensively cheerful, waves her hand*) Cheerioh.

(MISS GOSSAGE *exits, closing the door behind her*)

BILLINGS (*looking after her*) Any change'd be for the better. (*Despairingly*) No more news from the Ministry, I suppose, Miss Harper?

(TASSELL *takes a lighter from his pocket and lights Billings' and his own cigarette*)

JOYCE (*shaking her head*) None. Miss Whitchurch spoke to them this morning.

TASSELL (*cheerfully*) So did Pond. Same answer as usual. Receiving immediate attention. (*He examines another letter*)

BILLINGS (*bitterly*) It's been receiving that for the last three weeks. (*He gazes ahead*) Three weeks—of Audrey Thomson's gussets—sawdust in my bed—lunches consisting of cold hot-pot——

TASSEL (*reading a letter*) Greedy little blighter——

BILLINGS. Now, listen——

TASSELL. Not you. Hopcroft Mi.—writing home for another tin of Golden Syrup. He had a full one at tea-time yesterday.

WHITCHURCH (*off; calling*) Mr Pond.

BILLINGS (*in alarm*) Look out.

(BILLINGS *and* TASSELL *rise in a panic and drop their cigarettes into the flower vase.* TASSELL *moves to the fireplace,* BILLINGS *fans the smoke away with his hand.*
    MISS WHITCHURCH, *full of outraged indignation, enters up* R. JOYCE *rises*)

WHITCHURCH (*as she enters*) Where's Mr Pond? Where is he? (*She closes the door behind her*)

BILLINGS. He's in the study. (*Sarcastically*) He hoped you wouldn't mind.

(MISS WHITCHURCH *starts to cross to the door down* L *in a determined manner. Suddenly she pauses* L *of Billings*)

WHITCHURCH (*sniffing*) Something's burning.

BILLINGS. His ears, I expect. (*He perches himself on the* L *edge of the table* C)

WHITCHURCH (*sarcastically*) Ha, ha. (*She glares at Billings, moves to the door down* L *and calls*) Pond.

TASSELL (*moving* R *of the table* C) I think he's correcting prep.

WHITCHURCH (*turning*) I can't help that. He's got something else to correct now.

(*As she turns again to the door down* L POND *enters by it. He is startled to see* MISS WHITCHURCH *advancing on him and they almost collide*)

POND. Oh, I beg your pardon, Miss Whitchurch—I wasn't meaning to trespass——

WHITCHURCH. It's an outrage.

POND. Oh, come, come now—I seldom do use the study——

WHITCHURCH (*impatiently*) Never mind the study. (*She turns and moves* LC) A gross misdemeanour has been committed.

(JOYCE *takes a step forward*)

POND. Misdemeanour?

WHITCHURCH. Against my girls. And one of your boys was responsible.

POND. Good heavens!

BILLINGS. Which one of your girls was it?

WHITCHURCH. Not one—all of them.

POND. Good gracious!

BILLINGS. Good going.

JOYCE. What's happened exactly?

TASSELL. Or can't you tell us?

WHITCHURCH (*formidably*) Someone has punctured their back tyres.

Billings. Their what? (*To Tassell, disappointedly*) Oh—bicycles.

WHITCHURCH (*even more formidably*) And also tampered with their tool-bags.

POND. Tampered?

WHITCHURCH. With treacle.

POND. (*confused*) I thought you said with tool-bags.

WHITCHURCH (*exasperatedly*) With treacle and with tool-bags. A boy or boys has put treacle in the tool-bags of my girls.

(Pond, Billings and Tassel *all laugh.* Tassell *perches himself on the* R *edge of the table* C. Joyce *tries to conceal some amusement.* Pond *crosses to* R. *As he passes Billings and Tassell he gestures to them to stop laughing*)

Pond. Disgraceful—besides being a waste of treacle.

Billings *(still half-laughing)* In their tool-bags. That's a new one on me.

Tassell *(rising; involuntarily)* Golden syrup. Golden . . .

Whitchurch *(taking a step* R; *sharply)* I beg your pardon?

Tassell *(taking a step back; hastily)* I mean—of course, it might have been—on the other hand, of course, it probably wasn't.

Whitchurch. I see no significance one way or another. Both are equally glutinous.

Billings. Of course they are. *(To Tassell, frowning)* No significance at all.

Whitchurch. Unless, of course, it were a clue to the culprit. *(She moves in* L *of Billings)* Have you any idea who it could have been?

Billings. Us? Good Lord, no—none at all——

(Tassell *hastily picks up Hopcroft's letter and puts it in the envelope*)

(He looks at Tassell) Have we? *(He indicates to Tassell to seal the envelope)*

Tassell. Absolutely none. *(He licks the envelope and seals it)*

Whitchurch *(turning and moving* R *of Joyce)* Have you, Miss Harper?

(Tassell *and* Billings, *who rises, look anxiously at Joyce*)

Joyce. I? No—I haven't the faintest.

(Billings *and* Tassell *breathe a sigh of relief*)

Pond. Come to think of it, there's no proof that our boys had anything to do with it.

Billings *(perching himself again on the* L *edge of the table* C) Of course there isn't.

Whitchurch *(scornfully)* As if proof were needed. Who else would have done such a thing?

Pond. One of your girls might have.

Whitchurch. And treacle her own tool-bag. Poppycock. Besides, treacle isn't a girl's weapon. Is it, Miss Harper?

Joyce *(stepping forward a pace; honestly)* Well, as a matter of fact, Miss Whitchurch, I did know a case——

Whitchurch *(sharply)* That'll do, Miss Harper. *(She changes the subject)* Have the girls' letters been censored yet?

Joyce *(breaking slightly* L) They only began them after lunch.

Whitchurch. You'd better see if they've finished.

(Rainbow, *muttering resentfully and carrying a netball goal-post, passes from* R *to* L *across the outside of the french windows*)

Tassell (*crossing Billings and Miss Whitchurch to Joyce; hopefully*) I was just thinking—perhaps when I've finished mine, I might—help you with yours—when I've finished mine——

Joyce (*smiling*) That's very handsome of you.

Tassell (*eagerly*) Am I? I mean, is it? Then, can I?

Whitchurch (*intervening and touching Tassell on the arm*) I'm afraid *not*. (*Stiffly*) A young girl's disclosures are not always for masculine eyes.

(Tassell *crosses Miss Whitchurch to* R *of her, then turns*)

Tassell. Perhaps I could—(*he flips his tongue out and in quickly*) just lick the envelopes——

Whitchurch. If you desire to do so. Certainly.

Tassell. Oh, thanks awfully.

Joyce (*picking up her exercise-books and moving to the doors up* R) I'll get the letters immediately, Miss Whitchurch.

(Tassell *rushes to the doors up* C, *and holds one open for* Joyce, *who exits.* Tassell *closes the door behind her*)

Whitchurch (*to Pond*) Now, do you intend to track down the guilty party, or do you not?

Pond. I shall investigate the matter thoroughly. (*He sits in the easy chair above the fireplace*)

Whitchurch. At once?

Pond (*rising wearily*) If you insist.

Whitchurch. I do. What's more, I shall come with you.

(Tassell *opens the door up* R. Billings *rises*)

Pond (*moving to the doors up* R) Must you?

Whitchurch (*moving to the doors up* R) Yes, I must. This time we stick together.

(Pond *and* Miss Whitchurch *exit.* Tassell *closes the door*)

Billings (*standing* L *of the table* C) Disgusting.

Tassell (*moving to the fireplace*) What is?

Billings. Your Miss Harper business.

Tassell. What do you mean?

Billings (*disgustedly*) Lick her envelopes. You ought to be ashamed of yourself.

Tassell (*fervently*) She's the loveliest girl I've ever come across.

Billings. She's a St Swithin—that's enough for me.

Tassell. By name but not by nature. (*He moves* R *of the table* C) Look at the way she didn't rat on Hopcroft Mi.—there was nothing Swithinish about that.

Billings. The girl has some sporting instincts, I'll admit.

TASSELL (*moving to the fireplace*) The girl has everything. She has looks—she has charm—she has brains——

BILLINGS. And now, I suppose, you hope she'll have you.

TASSELL (*rapturously*) If only she would. (*He sits in the easy chair above the fireplace; worried*) The trouble is, I've got to work so fast. I'm scared stiff that before I have time to propose, the Ministry'll weigh in with a solution and off she'll go—out of my life for ever.

BILLINGS (*moving to the french windows*) That'll be the day.

TASSELL (*reproachfully*) Don't be a cad.

BILLINGS. I'm not. (*He turns*) All I want is to see the back of St Swithins. If your love life doesn't interfere with that—if youth calls to youth—(*he moves down* L) male calls to female—it's no concern of mine.

TASSELL (*meaningly*) I wouldn't be too sure.

BILLINGS (*turning quickly*) What d'you mean?

TASSELL. Miss Gossage. She's answered your call.

BILLINGS (*alarmed*) Don't be ridiculous.

TASSELL (*rising and moving* R *of the table* C) You don't mean to say you haven't noticed the symptoms?

BILLINGS (*more alarmed*) Symptoms——?

TASSELL. Look at all those flowers and what not——

BILLINGS (*moving* L *of the table* C; *aghast*) What? Queen Anne's Beard or whatever it is! Old Man's Lace? (*He leans across the table*) Don't tell me it means something in the language of flowers?

TASSELL. She's trying to show you how homey she can make your little nest.

BILLINGS (*wailing*) Nest? Don't say things like that. (*He slowly backs down* LC; *firmly*) You're trying to frighten me, that's what you're doing. If you think you can shift my attention from your treasonable passion for Miss Harper by raising these Gossage bogies, you're making a mistake. I haven't swallowed a word of it—not a single word——

(*His voice trails off as* MISS GOSSAGE *trips in up* R, *leaving the doors open. She is dressed for netball in abbreviated gym-dress, black stockings, white gym-shoes and a sash in the St Swithins colours. She runs with light steps down* R, *across to* L, *then runs round Billings and comes to attention* R *of him*)

GOSSAGE (*heartily*) Doesn't take *me* long to strip for games.

BILLINGS (*swallowing*) No—I can see that.

GOSSAGE. It must be very bracing here. (*She moves to the french windows and does physical jerks, facing off stage*) I feel chock-a-block full of energy this afternoon.

BILLINGS (*pseudo-heartily*) The sooner you pitch in and play it off the better.

GOSSAGE (*turning and doing bending exercises, facing the audience*) Oh—I've really got oodles of time——

Billings (*wincing*) Oodles.

Tassell (*collecting his letters together on the table*) Well, I've finished my little lot——

Billings (*hurrying to* L *of the table* C; *quickly*) No, no, don't go, old boy—— (*He indicates his letters*) I mean—look at all these I've got to stick up——

Gossage (*moving* L *of Billings; eagerly*) I'll lick your envelopes for you.

Billings (*turning to her*) What?

Tassell. Might as well face it now as later. (*He moves to the doors up* R) No good shutting your eyes to it. So long.

(Tassell *exits, closing the doors behind him.* Billings *looks after him in horror*)

Gossage (*crossing to the chair* R *of the table* C) Well—— (*She sits*) My tongue's hanging out.

Billings (*turning to her, startled*) What? Oh—no—as a matter of fact, thanks very much—now I come to look at them, they're all done—— (*He hurriedly scoops up the letters*)

Gossage (*leaning across the table*) What did Mr Tassell mean—no good shutting your eyes to it?

Billings. Oh! (*With a quick change of voice*) Well—er—when you're sticking envelopes, if you shut your eyes you might lick the address off the front or something—I'd better go and post these——

(*He turns to move to the doors up* R *but* Miss Gossage *rises quickly, cuts him off above the table* C *and takes the letters out of his hand*)

Gossage. No hurry—I'll drop them in, on my way . . . (*She places the letters on the table* C)

Billings (*defeated*) Thank you, Miss Gossage. (*He breaks down* L *of the table* C)

Gossage (*following him closely; warmly*) Call me Sausage.

Billings. Sausage?

Gossage. Gossage—Sausage. My nickname with the girls. (*Flatteringly*) I don't ask everyone to use it.

Billings (*appalled*) Oh. (*He crosses slowly down* R) Thank you very much.

Gossage (*following him*) I expect you've got a nickname too—with the boys?

Billings. Possibly. (*He is now facing his locker below the fireplace*)

Gossage (*still advancing*) Now don't pretend you don't know what it is. If you don't tell me, I shall only worm it out of one of them.

Billings. I shouldn't bother.

Gossage. Oh, yes I shall. (*She corners Billings. Roguishly*) Come on now, what is it? (*She grips his arm and twists him round to face her*)

BILLINGS (*looking down to evade her eye; disgustedly*) If you must know—Daisy.

GOSSAGE (*releasing him*) What an extraordinary nickname.

BILLINGS (*firmly*) And I don't ask anyone to use it.

GOSSAGE. Whatever made them call you Daisy?

BILLINGS. I was foolish enough in class one day to utter the words "Give me your answer do." (*Irritably*) Now, if you don't mind—— (*He makes to go*)

GOSSAGE (*holding up a reproving finger; reproachfully*) Daisy —temper—temper——

BILLINGS (*furiously*) Don't call me Daisy——

(MISS WHITCHURCH *and* POND *enter through the french windows from* R. MISS WHITCHURCH *is carrying a small empty Golden Syrup tin*)

WHITCHURCH (*triumphantly*) Caught! Red-handed!

BILLINGS (*indignantly*) Nothing of the sort.

WHITCHURCH (*moving* L *of the table* C) The tin was still inside his tuck-box—empty. (*She flourishes the tin*)

(POND *moves* L)

BILLINGS (*relieved*) Oh—the tool-bag treacler.

GOSSAGE (*running across between Miss Whitchurch and Pond to the french windows*) I must be off to netters.

(MISS GOSSAGE *exits up* L)

WHITCHURCH. As I predicted—a hooligan from Hilary Hall.

POND (*gloomily*) Hopcroft Minor. (*He sits in the easy chair* L)

BILLINGS (*nodding*) I know—good lad.

MISS WHITCHURCH *reacts and takes a step forward*)

(*Hastily*) I mean—good Lord! Are you sure?

POND. There was a trail of treacle—straight to his cubby hole.

WHITCHURCH. And what's more—traces on his person.

BILLINGS (*thoughtfully*) Hm. That does make it a bit sticky.

POND (*taking him literally*) He's washing them off now.

WHITCHURCH. The whole affair was a deliberate onslaught upon St Swithin's. I only hope an example will be made of it.

BILLINGS (*enthusiastically*) So do I.

POND (*nodding*) The boy fully deserves whatever reward——

(MISS WHITCHURCH *reacts violently*)

—*punishment*, we shall give him.

(*There is a knock at the door up* R)

(*He calls*) Yes?

(HOPCROFT *enters up* R, *closing the door behind him*)

(Genially) Ah, come in, Hopcroft. *(He pulls himself together and rises. Very severely)* Come in, boy.

(HOPCROFT *moves above the table* c)

First of all—your form master has something to say to you.

(HOPCROFT *moves down* R *of the table* c. BILLINGS *glares at Pond*)

BILLINGS *(looking down at Hopcroft)* Hopcroft, I'm surprised at you, being found out like that—*(hastily)* found out treacling tool-bags.
HOPCROFT. Yes, sir.
BILLINGS. You're old enough to know that that is *not* one of the uses of Golden Syrup.
HOPCROFT. Yes, sir.
BILLINGS. Glue would have been just as good——
WHITCHURCH *(interrupting, with heat)* We've had enough beating about the bush. I want corporal punishment.
BILLINGS *(eyeing her nastily)* How right you are. Isn't she, Headmaster?
POND. Quite. *(He crosses to* L *of Hopcroft)* Hopcroft—it will be our painful duty to chastise you.
BILLINGS. More painful for us than for you. *(To Pond)* I've said that before, but I've never meant it before.
WHITCHURCH *(moving* L *of Pond; impatiently)* Well—is there any more to be said?
POND. Nothing. *(He turns to Miss Whitchurch)* You can safely leave the rest to us.
WHITCHURCH. I hardly propose to carry out the sentence myself——
BILLINGS. Hardly.

(BILLINGS *and* POND *laugh*)

WHITCHURCH *(cutting into their laughter)* But I intend to witness the execution of it.
BILLINGS *(taken aback)* Oh, I don't think she could do that, could she?
POND. It would be highly improper.
BILLINGS *(to Miss Whitchurch)* You'd be surprised how improper.
WHITCHURCH *(icily)* I fail to see why.
BILLINGS. A young boy's disclosures are not always for feminine eyes.
WHITCHURCH *(defeated)* Very well. I bow to your judgement. *(She moves above the table* c, *then pauses)* I merely say this——

(POND *moves down* L)

(*She bangs the tin, in emphasis, on the back of the chair above the table*)
The boy must be punished most strongly on his deserts.

POND. On his where?

WHITCHURCH (*putting the tin on the table* C) What I mean is—
do not spare the rod. (*She moves to the doors up* R) And in future,
kindly keep your eyes on your pupils.

BILLINGS (*to Pond*) You'll need to see an oculist for that.

(MISS WHITCHURCH *glares at Billings, then exits up* R, *closing the
door behind her*)

POND (*moving to the small chair* LC *and sitting; genially*) Well,
Hopcroft, I don't want to be too severe——

(MISS WHITCHURCH *re-enters up* R)

WHITCHURCH. Six strokes at the very least.

POND. Only six? (*He nods and smiles at Miss Whitchurch, then
turns again to Hopcroft. Sternly*) As I was saying, Hopcroft, *I can't*
be too severe——

(MISS WHITCHURCH *exits up* R, *closing the door behind her*)

(*He rises and moves below the table* C. *In a friendly tone*) No—I can't
be *too* severe——

BILLINGS. Seeing it's your first offence——

POND. For today, at all events—— As a matter of fact, I don't
think I could lay my hand on the cane at the moment. Billings.
(*He beckons to Billings and moves to the french windows*)

(BILLINGS *crosses to Pond*)

What do you suggest, Billings?

(BILLINGS *whispers to* POND, *who shakes his head, then* POND
whispers to BILLINGS, *who shakes his head*)

BILLINGS. Fifty lines?

POND. Sounds rather a lot. We could keep him in, of course.

BILLINGS (*looking towards the french windows*) On a fine afternoon
like this?

POND. Well—just for a little while.

BILLINGS. Fifteen minutes?

POND. Ten, anyway.

BILLINGS. Right.

POND. That's settled then.

(BILLINGS *moves above the table* C)

(*He moves down* L. *To Hopcroft. Sternly*) Come here, boy.

(HOPCROFT *crosses to Pond*)

You realize, Hopcroft, that having committed an offence of this
kind, you must expect the very rigorous punishment it deserves?

HOPCROFT. Yes, sir.
POND. Very well. You will be kept in for five whole minutes.
HOPCROFT (*his face lighting up*) Thanks very much, sir.
POND. Thank *you* very much, Hopcroft.

(POND *bows to Hopcroft, turns and exits with great dignity down* L)

BILLINGS (*to Hopcroft*) Well—what are you waiting for?
HOPCROFT. I'm kept in for five minutes, sir.
BILLINGS. All right—you've been in five minutes, haven't you?
HOPCROFT (*puzzled*) Yes—I suppose I have, sir——
BILLINGS. Well then—run along and change.

(HOPCROFT *crosses below the table, then moves to the door up* R)
Hopcroft.

(HOPCROFT *stops up* R)

How's your pocket money going this week?
HOPCROFT (*turning to Billings*) It's gone, sir.
BILLINGS. What—all of it?
HOPCROFT. Yes, sir.
BILLINGS (*taking two half-crowns from his pocket*) Here's five bob. (*He holds the coins out to Hopcroft*)
HOPCROFT (*taking the money, astonished*) Thanks awfully, sir.
BILLINGS. And if you've—er—any more ideas of the same kind, don't get caught the next time.

(HOPCROFT *stares at him*)

HOPCROFT. No, sir.
BILLINGS. Well, cut along.

(*Completely astonished,* HOPCROFT *turns to the doors up* R. BILLINGS *moves to the french windows. They turn and look at each other.* BILLINGS *jerks his head and* HOPCROFT *exits up* R, *closing the door behind him.*

BILLINGS *takes a step outside the french windows. Looking off* L *he apparently sees something, turns in horror and exits hurriedly away outdoors to* R, *looking fearfully over his shoulder.*

After a moment, BARBARA *appears at the french windows from* L, *carrying a large bunch of turquoise-blue flowers. She looks after Billings for a moment, then peers in at the french windows to make sure the coast is clear.*

As she does so, TASSELL *enters up* R, *closing the door behind him. He is carrying some papers. He glances at Barbara, then moves to his locker above the fireplace and puts the papers away*)

BARBARA (*entering up* L) Oh—I just brought these for Miss Harper—I hope it's all right——
TASSELL (*turning*) I'll tell her. (*He moves* R *of the table* C)

BARBARA. Oh, no—they're anonymous—— (*She puts the flowers on the upstage end of the table* C)

TASSELL (*absently*) Looks more like larkspur to me. (*Realizing*) I see what you . . . (*Suddenly*) I say, it isn't her birthday, is it?

BARBARA. Miss Harper's? Heavens, no—that's December the fifth. (*She makes a mystic sign of the Zodiac in the air*) Sagittarius with Saturn in the ascendant. Lucky colour turquoise blue. (*She indicates the flowers*)

TASSELL (*moving slowly down* RC) You seem to know a lot about her private life.

BARBARA (*leaning on the back of the chair* LC; *seriously*) I've found out everything I can. (*Eagerly*) She's keen, isn't she?

TASSELL. Is she? What on?

BARBARA. Not on anything. Just keen. I think she's absolutely enormous. (*She eases down* L)

TASSELL (*stiffly*) I don't agree at all. She's very slim.

BARBARA (*scornfully*) I don't mean like that. I mean she's toasted cheese—ripe fruit—wizard, if you want to be old-fashioned.

TASSELL. Oh, thank you very much. Yes, I see what you mean.

BARBARA. Well, you do agree, don't you?

TASSELL (*in accents like hers*) Agree? I should say I do. (*He corrects himself and speaks normally*) I should say I do. I think Miss Harper's the most enormous thing I've ever seen.

(JOYCE *enters up* R, *carrying a quantity of envelopes. She closes the door behind her, puts the envelopes on the table* C *then moves* L *of it, staring at Tassell*)

(*Hastily*) Well—wizard, if you want to be old-fashioned. Oh, hullo, Miss Harper.

(JOYCE *smiles at him*)

JOYCE (*to Barbara*) What do you want, Barbara?

BARBARA (*gazing at her adoringly*) Me, Miss Harper? Oh—I just wanted to—well—I wondered if you'd let me help you with the envelopes——

TASSEL (*crossing below the table* C *to* R *of Joyce; indignantly*) Oh, now, look here—I was going to . . . I mean, bags I or whatever you call it.

JOYCE (*smiling; to Barbara*) Oughtn't you to be out at games?

TASSELL (*bending down to Barbara*) Yes, of course you ought —oughtn't you?

BARBARA (*retaliating*) I'm not playing today. Miss Gossage gave me two hour's garden weeding.

TASSELL. Well, go on then, pop out and pull up.

BARBARA (*pleadingly*) Oh, I say, Miss Harper, can't I——?

JOYCE (*firmly*) No, Barbara.

BARBARA (*very meekly*) Yes, Miss Harper.

(BARBARA *gazes adoringly at Joyce, then sighs, turns, and with a look at Tassell, runs to the french windows and exits to* L. JOYCE *follows her as far as the windows, then leans against the* R *side of them and looks after her*)

JOYCE (*smiling*) She's just at the worshipping age. I expect you suffer from the same kind of thing.

(TASSELL *moves to Joyce and stands down* L *of her, facing her*)

TASSELL (*looking at her ardently*) Yes—I think I do. Only much worse.

JOYCE. They soon grow out of it.

TASSELL. I doubt very much if I shall. I mean—er. (*He nearly kisses her, then seeing the flowers, he crosses to the table* C) Oh—these are for you. (*He picks up the flowers and turns*)

JOYCE (*surprised and touched*) Me? (*She moves to* L *of him and takes the flowers*) Oh—that's very nice of you——

TASSELL (*easing above the table* C) No, no—it isn't. They're larkspur—I mean, they're anonymous.

JOYCE (*smelling the flowers*) They're lovely—sort of turquoise blue.

TASSELL (*moving right of the table* C) Your lucky colour.

JOYCE (*surprised*) Is it? (*She starts to put the flowers in the vase on the table* C)

TASSELL (*nodding*) Sagittarius the fifth, with December in the ascendant—— (*He attempts a sign of the Zodiac in the air, but can't get it right*) I mean—— (*He gets carried away*) Miss Harper, if you only knew how keen I think I am—you are—that is—well, when I look at you—I think of toasted fruit and ripe cheese—— (*Emotionally*) Miss Harper——

JOYCE (*indicating the newly filled vase*) Would you put these on the mantelpiece, please.

(TASSELL *obediently takes the vase, places it on the upstage end of the mantelpiece, then returns to* R *of the table* C)

TASSELL. Oh, Miss Harper—I really must tell you——

JOYCE (*moving to the chair above the table* C) I think we'd better do the letters. (*She sits*)

TASSELL (*deflated*) Oh—yes—I suppose we had. (*He moves the chair* R *of the table* C *nearer to Joyce*)

(JOYCE *looks up*)

(*With an embarrassed smile*) It's—er—rather a long table for two. (*He sits rather suddenly in the chair* R *of the table* C) You won't have nearly so far to pass the envelopes now.

(JOYCE *smiles, opens the first letter and reads it.* TASSELL *studies Joyce's profile adoringly, hastily affecting an air of unconcern as she passes him the first letter and envelope. She picks up the next letter.*

TASSELL, *gazing at her again, absently folds the envelope in half, puts it inside the letter, folds the letter and licks the edge. He looks at it in bewilderment. They both laugh.* JOYCE *stops laughing and hands him the next letter and envelope, smiling very sweetly at him*)

(*Leaning forward; in a determined tone*) Miss Harper——

(POND *enters suddenly in great agitation down* L, *leaving the door open*)

POND (*crossing hurriedly below the table* C, *then to the doors up* R) Emergency! Emergency!

(TASSELL *sits back despairingly*)

Get everybody. There's no time to lose. (*He opens the doors up* R, *dashes into the hall, picks up the school bell and starts to ring it frantically*)

(TASSELL *and* JOYCE *look at each other in bewilderment, then turn in their chairs and look at Pond*)

(*He moves into the doorway still ringing the bell and shouts at Joyce and Tassell*) Don't sit there. Get everybody.

(TASSELL *and* JOYCE *both rise hurriedly, leaving some letters on the table.* JOYCE *picks up the others*)

TASSELL (*shouting above the noise of the bell*) What?
JOYCE (*shouting*) What's happened?
POND (*irritably*) I can't hear you.
TASSELL. What?

(POND *exasperatedly stops ringing the bell*)

POND (*agitatedly*) They'll be here in half an hour. Oh, fetch them in, can't you?
TASSELL. Fetch who?
JOYCE. Who'll be here? What's happened? (*She places the letters she has picked up, on the downstage* L *corner of the table* C, *then moves to the door down* L *and closes it*)
POND (*standing* L *of the doorway up* R; *exasperatedly*) Don't ask questions—there's no time.

(*He is about to ring the bell again when* MISS WHITCHURCH *enters hurriedly up* R. *She closes the* R *door*)

WHITCHURCH (*moving down to the fireplace sharply*) What's the meaning of this? Was that a boy's bell or a girl's bell?
POND. Neither—it's an alarm bell.

(BILLINGS *enters hurriedly through the french windows, and moves to* L *of the table* C)

BILLINGS. Are we on fire now?

(HOPCROFT *enters up* R, *half-changed—a cricket shirt hanging out of his white flannels. He closes the* L *door behind him*)

HOPCROFT (*excitedly*) I say, what's up? (*He sees the gathering of staff*) Oh, sorry, sir—— (*He turns to withdraw*)

POND (*catching Hopcroft by his shirt-tail*) No, Hopcroft—don't go. This emergency affects the entire school. *Both* entire schools.

WHITCHURCH. What emergency? Has this boy been at it again?

POND. No, *no.* Parents. Mr and Mrs Sowter. They've just telephoned me.

TASSELL (*aghast*) They haven't found out?

POND. Not yet. But it's only a matter of time. They're coming down here. Today. This afternoon.

BILLINGS. But didn't you tell 'em not to—invent something——?

POND. How could I? They're at the station. They're only waiting for a taxi. Oh, dang it, (*he involuntarily gives the bell a ring*) what can we do? (*He moves to the stool down R, and sits*)

TASSELL. Sowter? Aren't they the ones who don't want any feminine influence?

POND. Yes, yes—that only doubles the trouble. We must do something—what, I can't imagine——

HOPCROFT (*eagerly*) I know, sir—tell them we've all got scarlet fever.

WHITCHURCH. Since they telephoned? Don't be ridiculous. (*She takes hold of Hopcroft's right arm and slaps his hand*)

JOYCE (*easing LC*) You could say it had just broken out.

TASSELL. That's it—and then lock the main gate to prevent *them* breaking in.

POND (*with growing hope*) Lock the main gates—it's a possibility——

BILLINGS (*moving below the table C*) It isn't. If they even reach the main gates, what will they see through them? St Swithins netballing all over the playing field.

POND (*deflated*) So they will. No good.

(HOPCROFT *crosses above Tassell to the french windows*)

BILLINGS. There's only one thing to do. Eliminate St Swithins.

WHITCHURCH (*outraged*) Do what?

BILLINGS. Remove St Swithins from the scene. (*He crosses down L below Joyce*) Conceal the entire school while the Sowters are on the premises.

TASSELL. You mean, make them think we're still only Hilary Hall here?

BILLINGS. Of course.

TASSELL. By Jove! I believe R.B.'s right.

POND (*rising; seriously*) Fifty girls and three mistresses. We haven't enough cupboards to shut them up in.

WHITCHURCH (*moving forward a step; furiously*) I refuse to be shut up. I never heard of such a thing.

Pond. Come, come, Miss Whitchurch—you yourself spoke of co-operation——
Whitchurch. Co-operation. Not incarceration.
Tassell. It would only be for a couple of hours, at the most——
Whitchurch (*outraged*) A couple of hours—in a cupboard——
Billings (*crossing below Joyce to* LC) There's no question of cupboards. What's the position? The girls are playing netball—the boys are down at the baths. Right. All we have to do is to switch them over.
Joyce (*moving to Billings and placing her hand on his left arm*) You mean, send the girls down to the baths?
Billings (*nodding*) And bring the boys up to the playing fields. (*To Joyce and Miss Whitchurch*) You two and Miss Gossage keep out (*he throws Joyce's hand off his arm and moves to* L *of the table* C) of the way, and there you are.
Pond (*fervently*) Oh, I hope so.

(Joyce *breaks down* L)

Whitchurch (*dubiously*) I'm not at all sure I like the idea.
Billings. Nobody likes it. It's a matter of necessity.
Pond. After all, Hilary Hall would do the same for you. (*He makes signs to Billings and Tassell to support him*) Wouldn't we?
Billings. Obviously.
Tassell (*perching himself on the* R *edge of the table* C *and leaning towards Miss Whitchurch*) Of course we would.

(Billings, Tassell *and* Pond *look expectantly at Miss Whitchurch. There is a long pause while she looks at each of the masters in turn*)

Whitchurch. Oh, very well, then—under protest—yes.
Pond. Oh, thank you, Miss Whitchurch. I can't tell you what this means.

(Tassell *rises and moves above the table* C)

Billings. You can't now—we've got to get a move on.
Pond (*crossing below the table* C *to Hopcroft up* L) Yes, yes—Hopcroft—you go down to the baths, tell the boys to dry and dress with all speed and report to the pavilion instanter.
Hopcroft. Yes, sir——

(Hopcroft *exits through the french windows and runs off to* L)

Pond. Tassell—you'll take the cricket, of course, when they get there.

(Tassell *nods*)

(*He turns to Joyce*) Miss Harper, perhaps you'd . . .
Whitchurch (*crossing below the table and Billings to Joyce; with*

umbrage) Miss Harper is on *my* staff. She takes her instructions from me.

POND. Then kindly give them.

WHITCHURCH. Miss Harper——

POND. Get your girls off the playing field and down to the baths.

WHITCHURCH. Miss Harper——

BILLINGS. Undressed and under water instanter.

WHITCHURCH. Miss Harper——

TASSELL. Instanter.

WHITCHURCH (*glaring*) Tell Miss Gossage . . .

JOYCE. All right—I know what.

(JOYCE *turns, moves to the french windows and exits.* POND, BILLINGS *and* TASSELL *are sniggering*)

WHITCHURCH (*scathingly*) The laughter of fools is like the crackling of thorns under a pot.

(RAINBOW *enters up* R *leaving the doors open*)

POND (*crossing Billings to below the table* C) Don't stand there, Billings—go immediately.

RAINBOW (*moving* R *of the table* C) Beg pardon, sir——

POND (*irritably*) What is it, Rainbow?

RAINBOW. I heard the bell go.

POND (*alarmed*) The bell. Not the Sowters?

TASSELL. Can't be.

RAINBOW. I was in the grounds. I heard it go. But when I come—it's gone.

POND (*agitatedly*) Come—gone—what are you talking about?

WHITCHURCH. That man talks in riddles. I can never solve him. Rainbow, if the front door went . . .

BILLINGS (*suddenly realizing*) He doesn't (*he nods towards the door*) mean that one. He means *that* one. (*He shakes the bell Pond is holding*)

POND. Oh, this one. (*He hands the bell to Rainbow*) That was me.

RAINBOW (*giving Pond a look*) Beg your pardon, sir. (*He turns and moves to the doors up* R)

(POND *crosses to the fireplace.* BILLINGS *eases up* L)

TASSELL (*moving up* RC; *urgently*) Wait a minute—Rainbow—the playing field—it's fixed up for netball, I suppose?

RAINBOW (*bitterly*) It is. And the game I had with them contraptions——

WHITCHURCH (*severely*) They're not contráptions—they're goals.

RAINBOW (*disbelievingly*) Goals? Ten foot up in the air, with busted butterfly nets hanging off of them.

POND (*exasperatedly*) Oh, never mind the butterflies—change it over immediately—cricket is going to be played. (*He takes the bell from Rainbow, moves into the hall and restores it to its place*)

RAINBOW. Cricket? But—— (*He nods at Miss Whitchurch*) It's their turn.

BILLINGS (*impatiently*) They're missing a turn.

TASSELL (*pushing Rainbow to the french windows; urgently*) Netball's off—cricket's on—straight away—*now*.

RAINBOW (*moving unwillingly; aghast*) Now? But I've just put in them contraptions.

POND (*re-entering and moving R of the table C; desperately*) Don't argue, Rainbow—rectify.

RAINBOW. Yes, sir. (*As he goes*) I always said it wasn't feasible . . .

(RAINBOW *exits through the french windows, muttering*)

TASSELL (*moving to the doors up R*) I must get changed.

(TASSELL *exits hurriedly, leaving the doors open.* BILLINGS *eases above the table* C)

POND. Billings—you'd better go through the school, looking for girls.

WHITCHURCH (*crossing below the table C to the doors up R*) I will do that, thank you. If there *are* any odd girls . . .

BILLINGS. Plenty.

WHITCHURCH. They will be out of the way before many minutes are passed.

POND. And before any Sowters are present.

WHITCHURCH. Yes.

(MISS WHITCHURCH *gives Pond a look and exits up* R, *closing the doors*)

POND. I must go and change myself.

BILLINGS (*puzzled*) You're not going to play cricket too?

POND. No, no—into my academicals—the Sowters are the sort to expect it. You keep an eye on the drive——

BILLINGS. They won't be here yet, will they?

POND. I hope to goodness not. Still, it's best to be on the safe side.

(POND *exits up* R)

BILLINGS *shrugs his shoulders then also exits up* R, *closing the doors behind him.*

A moment later, MRS PECK, *carrying a handbag, an umbrella and a small parcel, appears from* L *outside the french windows and, after peering rather nervously in, enters the room. She is a small, thin, rather old-fashioned woman of about fifty. She is followed by* THE REVEREND EDWARD PECK, *who is carrying a raincoat, gloves, a box of sweets and a newspaper. He is an earnest man dressed in light clerical grey. He is about the same age as his wife. Both have a mild,*

almost nervous manner. He is about to pass the window when
Mrs Peck *calls softly*)

Mrs Peck. Edward.

(Mr Peck *stops and peers in the window*)

This looks like the staff side, dear. I'm afraid we've come in the
back way. (*She moves a little down* lc)

Mr Peck (*entering the room and looking around*) Dear me—so
we must have. Never mind—I'm sure Miss Whitchurch will for-
give us. (*He moves* l *of the table* c) They seem to have found quite
pleasant quarters.

Mrs Peck. They do. I was afraid, as Julia hadn't said very
much in her letters——

Mr Peck. Yes, yes—I'd better try and find someone——
(*He turns*)

(*As he does so,* Barbara *passes the french windows. She is wearing
an old glove on her right hand and is carrying a short-handled hoe*)

Ah—— (*He calls to Barbara*) Excuse me—— (*He moves to the french
windows*)

(Barbara *stops, then enters the room*)

I—ah—I don't know your name, I'm afraid——

Barbara. Barbara Cahoun. *Not* spelt Colquhoun. You're Mr
and Mrs Peck, aren't you? (*She stands between them*)

Mrs Peck (*nodding*) Julia's parents. How clever of you.

Mr Peck. We were looking for Miss Whitchurch. (*He eases
down* lc) You see, we suddenly decided to come down . . .

Barbara (*staring*) Do you mean she didn't know you were
coming?

Mrs Peck. No. It's quite a surprise visit.

Barbara. Gosh! It certainly will be. I say, what a piece of
gruesome.

Mrs Peck. A piece of what, dear?

Barbara. I mean a smack in the eye. I'd better find her right
away. (*She runs to the door down* l, *knocks, and opening it, peers off*)
Not in there. Won't be a sec.——

(Barbara *runs across to the doors up* r *and exits, closing the doors
behind her.* Mr *and* Mrs Peck *look at one another, bewildered*)

Mrs Peck (*a little sadly*) Why should we be a smack in the eye?

Mr Peck. I don't know, dear. Or a bit of gruesome.

(Tassell, *wearing cricket shirt and flannels, and carrying his
blazer, enters up* r *closing the doors behind him. He is a little startled
at seeing the Pecks, but quickly puts on a winning smile*)

Tassell. Oh—good afternoon. (*He moves* r *of the table* c) You
managed to get here very quickly——

Mrs Peck. Well—I'd hardly say that——

Tassell (*smiling*) Excuse me, won't you—they're waiting for me to start the game. (*He moves to his locker above the fireplace, opens it and takes out his cricket boots, picks up the cricket bat from the corner up* R, *and puts them with his blazer on the upstage end of the table* C)

(Mr *and* Mrs Peck *stare at him, look at one another, puzzled, then look again at* Tassell)

(*He turns to them. Extra heartily*) I expect you'll be out later to watch the cricket. We've got a pretty good team this term. I've been putting them through it thoroughly down at the nets. (*He moves above the table to* R *of Mr Peck*)

Mrs Peck (*a little taken aback*) Putting them through it?

Tassell. Rather. You needn't worry about mollycoddling here, I assure you. Cold bath every morning—a good stiff run twice a week—boxing—— (*He takes up a boxing stance*) Fencing—— (*He takes up a fencing stance*) I'm a great believer in knocking the nonsense out of them right from the start.

Mrs Peck. So it seems.

Mr Peck. You—er—you're on the staff here?

Tassell. Oh yes, rather. (*He moves to the table* C, *where he starts loosening the laces of his cricket boots*)

Mrs Peck. Couldn't they get anyone else?

Tassell (*taken aback*) I beg your pardon?

Mrs Peck. A mistress, I mean. To do your work?

Tassell (*turning; indignantly*) They didn't want a mistress.

Mrs Peck. How very strange. (*To Mr Peck*) Isn't it, dear?

Mr Peck (*nodding*) This is quite an innovation. (*To Tassell*) Miss Gossage has gone, I take it——

Tassell (*bewildered*) Miss Gossage——

Mrs Peck. I don't understand Miss Whitchurch making no attempt to get a mistress——

Mr Peck (*nodding*) She's always been so much against turning the girls into tomboys.

Tassell. Turning the . . . You *are* Mr and Mrs Sowter, aren't you?

Mr Peck. No, no—our name's Peck.

Tassell (*staring at him*) Peck—— (*He steps back a pace*) I thought there was something funny when I saw you were a . . . I mean—— (*He puts his hand to his neck where his collar would be*)

Mr Peck. Something funny?

Mrs Peck (*apologetically*) I suppose we should have warned Miss Whitchurch. We're Julia's parents.

Tassell (*playing up*) Oh, Julia's parents. (*He picks up his blazer and puts it on*) Of course, how silly of me. Dear little Julia Peck. (*He moves below the table* C *to the fireplace*)

Mrs Peck (*with pride*) Well—she's five feet four, you know.

Tassell. Oh, I know—yes, dear, large, little Julia Peck.

(BILLINGS *enters up* R, *closing the door behind him*)

BILLINGS (*as he enters*) No sign of those blasted parents yet. (*He suddenly sees the Pecks, reacts violently, moves above the table* C *and hurriedly tries to manage a polite smile*) Oh, how d'you do? My name's Billings. (*He moves* L *of the table* C *and holds out his hand to Mr Peck*) I'm . . .

TASSELL (*moving below the table* C *and intervening quickly*) The school doctor.

BILLINGS (*startled*) What?

TASSELL (*to Billings*) Mr and Mrs Peck—parents of Julia Peck. One of the biggest girls in St Swithins. (*He moves up* C, *passing between Billings and the table* C)

BILLINGS (*turning in horror to Tassell*) St—oh!

TASSELL (*to Mr Peck*) Dr Billings is new this term too, of course. (*He moves* R *of the table* C)

MR PECK. What happened to Dr Gunn?

TASSELL. Gunn? Oh, he went off very suddenly.

(MRS PECK *crosses below Mr Peck and holds out her hand to Billings*)

BILLINGS. How d'you do?

MRS PECK. I'm very pleased to meet you, Doctor. I don't need to tell you that Julia is rather a delicate girl.

(MR PECK *moves to the pegs* L, *hands up his hat and coat, then moves to the french windows and stands looking out over the grounds*)

BILLINGS (*bitterly*) She would be. At her age, I mean.

(TASSELL *moves to the fireplace*)

MRS PECK. Her stamina is so small.

(BILLINGS *pulls the chair* L *of the table* C *towards him, and stands in a doctor's attitude with one foot up on the seat of the chair*)

BILLINGS. I've noticed that. Curious when the rest of her is so large.

MRS PECK. She seems to have very little resistance.

BILLINGS (*sympathetically*) Well, of course, there are a lot of girls like that.

MRS PECK. She cycled too much last term and in the end she got run down.

BILLINGS. In which end? I mean—did she? Run down? Very unpleasant. Who by?

MRS PECK (*puzzled*) By herself, I suppose.

BILLINGS (*taking his foot off the chair*) Sounds a funny sort of accident. (*He returns the chair to* L *of the table* C) Ah, well, never mind, she won't be doing any bicycling for a while.

MRS PECK. Ah, you've seen to that?

BILLINGS. No—but someone else has.

(TASSELL *moves* R *of the table* C. MR PECK *turns and moves slowly down* L)

MRS PECK (*anxiously*) I hope, Doctor, you haven't allowed *her* to take part in any of these rough games.

BILLINGS. Rough games? At St Swithins? You can't know Miss Whitchurch. She won't even allow the girls to . . .

(*He breaks off and stares at* TASSELL, *who is shaking his head and finger violently, and making "Psst" noises.* MR PECK *sees Tassell and draws* MRS PECK'S *attention to him.* TASSELL *converts his signals into "involuntary twitch"*)

TASSELL (*still twitching and backing to the fireplace; apologetically*) It's a sort of nervous twitch I've got, Doctor. I'd like a word with you about it. (*He stops twitching and turns to the fireplace*)

MR PECK (*concerned*) It doesn't seem a very healthy neighbourhood.

BILLINGS (*turning to the Pecks*) Far from healthy. In fact, I don't advise you to stay a moment longer than you need.

MRS PECK (*worried*) Really? Then it doesn't seem very wise to have moved the school here.

(MISS WHITCHURCH *enters anxiously up* R, *closes the doors behind her, and moves down* R *of the table* C)

WHITCHURCH (*aghast as she sees the group*) Oh, I'm too late.

BILLINGS. Too late to introduce us, yes.

TASSELL. We've done it for ourselves.

(MISS WHITCHURCH *crosses below the table* C *to Mr and Mrs Peck and shakes hands with them.* BILLINGS *crosses above the table* C *and joins Tassell at the fireplace*)

MR PECK. It was something of a surprise, Miss Whitchurch, but I suppose what must be must be.

WHITCHURCH. I'm glad you can take it that way, very glad indeed. Of course, I'm taking steps to part company with the boys at the earliest possible moment.

(BILLINGS *and* TASSELL *react to each other at this*)

MRS PECK. The boys?

TASSELL (*moving below the table* C; *hurriedly laughing it off*) Miss Whitchurch calls us that for short. (*He turns gaily to Miss Whitchurch*)

(MISS WHITCHURCH *freezes him with her expression*)

I—er—was (*he backs down* R) going to explain to Mr and Mrs Peck that my position as games master is purely temporary.

BILLINGS (*moving* R *of the table* C) And mine—filling the—er—breach left by Dr Gunn. (*As he returns to the fireplace he repeats to Miss Whitchurch*) Doctor Gunn.

WHITCHURCH (*grasping the situation*) Oh. Oh, quite.

MRS PECK (*to Miss Whitchurch*) We were a little worried about Julia—that's why we came down so early in the term.

WHITCHURCH. Worried?

MRS PECK. Her letters, Miss Whitchurch. They didn't seem as frank as usual.

WHITCHURCH. Strange. (*As she speaks, she sees the pile of letters on the downstage end of the table c and slides the needlework over them, while still facing the Pecks*) Of course, I don't know how frank they used to be.

MRS PECK. We thought she might be hiding something from us.

WHITCHURCH. Oh, I hardly think that. After all, what could there be to hide?

(POND *enters up* R, *closing the doors behind him. He is wearing his best suit, wing collar, his mortar-board and gown with full academic honours. He enters with an expansive smile*)

POND. Ah—*good* afternoon. (*He stops abruptly, the smile freezing on his face*)

MR PECK. Good heavens.

(MR PECK *backs down* L. MRS PECK *follows him.* BILLINGS, *coming to the rescue, moves to Pond and, laughing heartily, slaps him on the back*)

BILLINGS (*clapping his hands*) Very good indeed. A first-class impersonation, isn't it, Tassell?

(TASSELL *gets a vague idea and claps his hands weakly*)

(*To the Pecks, as he pushes the somewhat reluctant Pond down stage*) Mr Pond's playing the star part in the end-of-term theatricals. *Eric, or Little by Little.*

(POND *is between Tassell and Billings*)

TASSELL. He had to start rehearsing already—very slow at learning his lines.

MR PECK. Mr Pond? I don't think we've met——?

POND. No.

(*Before Pond can continue,* BILLINGS *grabs his left arm and stops him*)

BILLINGS (*quickly*) Ah, I don't suppose so. You see, they were married in the holidays.

MRS PECK. Married? Who?

BILLINGS. Mr. Pond and Miss Whitchurch.

TASSELL. That's only her trade name now. (*He pushes Pond across to* R *of Miss Whitchurch, then backs down* R. *To Miss Whitchurch*) Isn't it, Mrs Pond?

WHITCHURCH (*gulping*) Well—er—yes.

(Miss Whitchurch *and* Pond *stand side by side, highly uncomfortable.* Billings *moves to the fireplace, and leans his head on the mantelpiece*)

Mr Peck. This *is* a surprise.
Pond. I should say so—suppose so.
Mrs Peck. Congratulations.
Mr Peck. Yes, indeed.

(Mrs Peck *turns to* Mr Peck *and they discuss the matter smilingly. While their attention is diverted,* Pond *looks helplessly at Miss Whitchurch*)

Pond (*in an undertone*) Who the dickens——?
Whitchurch (*also in an undertone; forcefully*) *My* parents.
Pond (*surprised*) Yours? Oh, really. (*He moves to the Pecks*) Well, this *is* an unexpected pleasure. (*He shakes hands with Mr Peck*) How d'you do, sir? (*He turns to Mrs Peck*) And—er—— (*He removes his mortar-board*)

(Mrs Peck *extends her hand*)

(*Shyly*) May I call you Mother? (*He kisses her on the cheek*)

(Mrs Peck *is amazed.* Mr Peck *stares, outraged. The others look astonished*)

(*He continues happily*) You mustn't feel you've lost your daughter—but rather gained a son.
Mrs Peck (*aghast*) Lost our daughter?
Pond. Perhaps one day we shall bring you back the patter of little feet.
Mr Peck. What?
Billings (*moving* R *of the table* C; *hurriedly*) It's quite all right, sir. (*To Mrs Peck*) Nothing to worry about, Mrs Peck. Mr Pond took you for his wife's mother.

(Pond *is horrified*)

Mrs Peck (*taking umbrage*) Well, really—— (*She moves* L *of Miss Whitchurch*) I know I'm not so young as I was, but I'm hardly old enough to be . . .
Whitchurch (*icily*) Hardly old enough to be *what*, Mrs Peck?

(Mrs Peck *retreats to* L *of Mr Peck. Before the storm can break,* Hopcroft *enters through the french windows, rather breathless. He hurries down between Pond and Miss Whitchurch*)

Hopcroft (*to Pond*) I've told them, sir—they're all on their way up.
Whitchurch (*aghast*) What?
Hopcroft (*to Pond*) They thought I was ragging at first, but I told them . . .
Pond (*hurriedly*) That'll do, that'll do. Be off with you.

(*He bundles* Hopcroft *to the french windows.* Hopcroft *exits to* L)

Mrs Peck (*a little bewildered by the speed of the event; crossing to* R *of Mr Peck*) Who was that?

Pond (*returning to his original position* R *of Miss Whitchurch, unthinkingly*) One of my boys. (*Hastily*) One of *our* boys. (*He takes hold of Miss Whitchurch's right arm*) Er—the eldest, of course.

Mr Peck. But I thought you were only married in the holidays?

Tassell (*moving above the table* C) He may be slow at some things, but he's very quick at others.

(*Faint sounds of boys' voices are heard off.* Tassell *hears them and eases to the french windows*)

Billings (*following Tassell to the french windows*) The holidays fifteen years ago, it was—in Australia.

(Tassell *stands* L *of the french window opening, with* Billings R *of him*)

Mrs Peck. Australia?

Billings (*blandly*) Yes—that accounts for your not having run into the family before.

(Mr Peck *turns and eases towards the french windows*)

Tassell. They've only just come up over from down under.

(*The sound of boys' voices grows louder.* Pond *and* Miss Whitchurch *move hastily to the french windows and fill the rest of the gap*)

Mr Peck (*trying to see out of the french windows*) Gracious me. A lot more boys.

(*He tries to get a closer look, but* Pond, Miss Whitchurch, Billings *and* Tassell *interpose themselves by dodging from side to side*)

Billings (*as he tries to obscure the view*) It's a very large family.

Tassell. Fifteen years, you know, and several sets of twins.

(*They effectively prevent Mr Peck from being able to see out. The boys' voices die away*)

Whitchurch (*taking Mr Peck's arm and leading him down* L; *quickly*) Well, I mustn't keep you standing here. If you'd care to come into my study, Mr Peck—— (*Frigidly to Mrs Peck*) And Mrs Peck, of course.

(Mr Peck *moves to the pegs* L *and takes down his hat and coat*)

Mrs Peck (*mildly*) We'd like to see Julia as soon as possible.

Whitchurch (*moving to the door down* L; *firmly*) Quite. But this

is a little too soon. She's down at the baths—up in the bathroom
—er—having a bath.

Mr Peck (*surprised*) After luncheon?

Billings (*moving down* R *of Mrs Peck; quickly*) I prescribed it—
three times a day after meals.

Mrs Peck. That would be for her pores, I expect.

Billings (*blandly*) Oh no—not just her (*he holds out his hands*)
paws—all over.

Mr Peck (*a little bewildered*) Perhaps we could wander round
the grounds. (*He half turns towards the french windows*)

(Billings *intercepts him*)

Pond (*shaking his head*) No, no—for the present—out of bounds.

Whitchurch. The girls are playing hare and hounds.

(Miss Whitchurch *opens the door down* L *and exits with the
Pecks*)

Pond (*sitting in the easy chair* L; *agitatedly*) Here's a nice how
d'you do. I shall need the study myself in a few minutes for the
Sowters.

(Rainbow, *muttering resentfully and carrying a netball goal-post,
passes from* L *to* R *across the outside of the french windows*)

Tassell (*moving* L *of the table* C *and looking towards the door down* L
in sudden alarm) Supposing they see things—Hilary Hall reports,
and what not?

Pond (*definitely*) He's a parson—he wouldn't look—— (*Dubiously*) Would he?

Billings (*easing down* LC; *looking at the door down* L) Well, I
knew a bishop once, who was quite capable .

(Miss Whitchurch *enters hurriedly down* L, *closing the door
behind her. She is surprised to see the three masters still there*)

Whitchurch. Haven't you organized it?

Pond. Organized what?

Whitchurch. The change-over, of course. Boys back to baths
—girls to playing field. (*She moves to the french windows*) I'll see to
it.

Pond (*rising; agitatedly*) Here—no—stop—I say, you can't do
that. You musn't.

Whitchurch (*turning to him; forcefully*) I can, I must, and I
will.

Pond. But the Sowters—they'll be here any minute.

Whitchurch. They aren't here now. The Pecks are. First
come—first served.

Billings (*forcefully*) Yes, but people in glass houses should not
throw stones.

Whitchurch. What has that to do with it?

BILLINGS (*defeated*) I don't know. (*He breaks down* L *and leans against the downstage lintel of the door down* L)

WHITCHURCH. Nincompoop. (*Forcefully, to Pond*) You can meet your Sowters down the road, tell them the drive's up, and divert them through the tradesmen's entrance—then put them in the servants' hall.

POND (*horrified*) Sowters in the servants' hall?

WHITCHURCH. Tell them it's the temporary waiting-room. And when you've done so, all of you and the boys will go to the baths, sending the girls up here.

POND. *All* go?

TASSELL ⎱ (*together*) What, us?
BILLINGS ⎰

(TASSELL *moves to* R *of Miss Whitchurch,* BILLINGS *to* L *of Pond*)

WHITCHURCH. I'm risking no further imbroglios such as we've had already.

BILLINGS (*dryly*) So we have to leave the Sowters in the servants' hall, without even a guard on the door to see they stay inside?

WHITCHURCH. Lock them in, and tell them later the door jammed.

POND. But that's ridiculous.

WHITCHURCH. Those are my terms. It's either that, or exposure.

TASSELL. Then we'll make it double exposure.

POND (*in agitation*) Oh—what is all this? It's no time to talk photography.

WHITCHURCH. Will you do it, or won't you?

POND (*helplessly to Billings and Tassell*) Will we or won't we?

TASSELL. We'll jolly well have to.

BILLINGS (*to Miss Whitchurch as he moves the small chair from* LC *up to* R *of the french windows*) But only if you pack those Pecks off as fast as you can.

WHITCHURCH (*turning to Billings; with umbrage*) I shall naturally do my utmost——

(RAINBOW *passes the french windows. At the same moment* BARBARA *enters up* R. TASSELL *sees Rainbow simultaneously with* MISS WHITCHURCH *seeing Barbara*)

TASSELL ⎱ (*together*) ⎱Rainbow.
WHITCHURCH ⎰ ⎰Barbara.

(TASSELL *moves towards Rainbow and bumps into* MISS WHITCHURCH *who moves towards Barbara.* RAINBOW *enters at the french windows,* BARBARA *closes the doors and moves above the table* C)

TASSELL ⎱ (*together*) ⎰Rainbow . . .
WHITCHURCH ⎰ ⎰Barbara . . .

(TASSELL *and* MISS WHITCHURCH *bump again.* BILLINGS *intervenes, pulls Tassell up stage and gestures to Miss Whitchurch*)

BILLINGS (*blandly*) Shall we try it one at a time? (*He turns and leans on the bookcase, with his back to the audience*)

(RAINBOW *waits with a long-suffering expression on his face*)

WHITCHURCH. Barbara——
BARBARA. Yes, Miss Whitchurch?
WHITCHURCH. Find Miss Harper and ask her to come up here at once. Tell her Mr and Mrs. Peck are here.
BARBARA. Yes, Miss Whitchurch.

(BARBARA *dodges past Tassell, Billings and Rainbow and exits through the french windows.* MISS WHITCHURCH *nods frigidly to Tassell*)

TASSELL (*crossing to* L *of the easy chair up* R) Rainbow. It's about the playing field——
RAINBOW (*crossing to* L *of Tassell*) It's all ready for you. Them contraptions. They're harder to take out than what they are to put in.
TASSELL. That's a good thing. You've got to put them in again.
RAINBOW. I've got to what?
TASSELL. Change it all back again to netball—quick as you can. The boys are going back to the baths.

(MR PECK *enters down* L)

RAINBOW. But you said cricket was going to be . . .
POND. Don't argue.
MR PECK. Excuse me——
POND (*turning towards Mr Peck; fiercely*) Shut up. (*He sees who it is*) Oh, I beg your pardon.
MR PECK (*smiling nervously*) Er—my wife was wondering . . .
WHITCHURCH (*crossing to Mr Peck; firmly*) I'm afraid not, Mr Peck. Not *yet*. I'd like you to look through the summer science syllabus.

(MISS WHITCHURCH *hustles* MR PECK *and follows him off down* L, *closing the door behind her*)

POND (*moving* L *of the table* C) Well, don't stand there, Rainbow —this is urgent.
RAINBOW (*rebelliously*) The opposite was ten minutes ago. I might just as well wait another ten minutes and . . .
POND (*outraged*) Rainbow.
RAINBOW (*resignedly*) Very good, sir. (*With an awful look he moves to the doors up* R, *then pauses and turns*) I'm going to put my tea kettle on first.

(RAINBOW *dares them by his look to disagree, then turns and exits up* R, *closing the doors behind him.* TASSELL *moves to the fireplace*)

POND. That man's becoming mutinous. (*He moves* R *of the table* C)

BILLINGS (*crossing to* L *of the easy chair* R) Never mind Rainbow—we'd better see about the Sowters.

TASSELL (*sitting on the stool down* R) We can't lock them in——

BILLINGS. Of course not. (*To Pond*) You'll have to ask them to wait and hope to goodness they'll wait long enough.

POND (*sitting in the easy chair* R) But suppose they don't—they might wander round the grounds——

TASSELL. With netball in full swing.

BILLINGS. I've been thinking about that. We can't risk St Swithins coming up at all. We'll tell that Sausage woman she's to take the girls for a walk.

TASSELL. A nice long walk.

BILLINGS. They can go out at the bottom gate, by the baths. Phew! I could do with a cold plunge myself.

POND. Hear, hear.

(POND *is about to rise, when* TASSELL *rises hurriedly, moves to Pond and puts his left hand on Pond's right shoulder, so that* POND *is half-standing, half-sitting*)

TASSELL (*suddenly*) Listen.
BILLINGS. What?
TASSELL. I believe I can hear a car.
POND ⎱
BILLINGS⎰ (*together; aghast*) What?
TASSELL. Sh! Listen.

(*They all listen intently for a moment*)

BILLINGS. Oh, heavens.
POND. The Sowters.

(*First* BILLINGS, *then* POND, *and lastly* TASSELL *exit hurriedly up* R, *leaving the doors open.*
RAINBOW *enters through the french windows*)

RAINBOW (*as he enters*) I just thought of another thing—— (*He breaks off as he finds the room empty, shrugs resignedly and turns to the french windows*)

(*As he does so,* HOPCROFT *comes down the stairs and enters up* R, *closing the doors behind him*)

HOPCROFT (*in the doorway; in an undertone*) Hi—Rainbow.
RAINBOW (*turning and crossing to Hopcroft; despairingly*) If you got another message from the Head . . .
HOPCROFT. I haven't. (*He takes Rainbow by the right arm, leads*

him down RC *and speaks conspiratorially*) How'd you like to earn half a crown?

RAINBOW (*suspiciously*) I'd have to see it first.

(HOPCROFT *takes half a crown from his pocket and shows it*)

What would I have to do?

HOPCROFT. Go down to the baths and pinch all their clothes.

RAINBOW. And play fast and loose with my bread-and-butter? No, thank you. (*He crosses below the table to the french windows*)

HOPCROFT (*kicking the rug; exasperatedly*) Oh, hang! And now was just the time to finish them off for good and all.

RAINBOW (*pausing and turning*) Finish who?

HOPCROFT. St Swithins, of course.

(RAINBOW's *face lights up. He rubs his hands with pleasure and crosses to Hopcroft*)

RAINBOW. St Swithins? Why didn't you say so before?

HOPCROFT (*eagerly*) You'll do it, then?

RAINBOW (*thoughtfully*) Yes, but wait a minute—it don't make sense to me—going down and pinching . . . How's that going to finish off St Swithins?

HOPCROFT (*impatiently*) It's obvious how.

RAINBOW (*perplexed*) Is it?

HOPCROFT. Of course it is. But there's no time to stand here gassing. (*He holds out the half-crown on the palm of his hand*) Will you do it, or won't you?

RAINBOW (*grimly*) I'll try anything once. (*He reaches for the coin*)

HOPCROFT. Good egg. (*He closes his hand over the coin and withdraws it*) I'll pay you afterwards. (*He turns and runs to the doors up* R)

RAINBOW (*turning and following Hopcroft*) Here—wait a minute.

(HOPCROFT *stops and turns*)

I never known your sort go flinging half-crowns away. What's the idea of getting *me* to do it?

HOPCROFT (*with an air of innocence*) Well, if you do it, I can't get caught, can I?

RAINBOW. No, I suppose . . . What? Now listen . . .

HOPCROFT (*suddenly*) Look out—scram.

(HOPCROFT *exits hurriedly up* R, *leaving the doors open.*
     RAINBOW, *slower in the uptake, is looking after Hopcroft as* MISS WHITCHURCH *and the* PECKS *enter down* L. RAINBOW *turns*)

WHITCHURCH (*moving up* L) I dare say now that the girls . . . (*She is dismayed to see Rainbow. Severely*) Rainbow, haven't you done yet that which you have to do?

(MR PECK *moves to the up* L *corner of the table* C. MRS PECK *stands by the down* L *corner of the table* C)

RAINBOW (*defensively*) I was only told five minutes ago . . .

WHITCHURCH (*hastily*) I know what you were told. I want to see results.

RAINBOW (*looking straight at her*) Don't worry, mum, you're going to.

(RAINBOW *gives her a nasty look, crosses below her and exits through the french windows*)

MR PECK. You were saying, Miss Whitchurch, about the girls——?

WHITCHURCH. I was saying I dare say now that the girls are —er—well on their way home. They've been out for a nature study ramble.

MR PECK (*puzzled*) I thought you said they were playing hare and hounds.

WHITCHURCH (*stiffly*) Nature study embraces flora *and fauna*.

MRS PECK. And what about Julia?

WHITCHURCH. I beg your pardon?

MRS PECK (*plaintively*) Won't she be out of her bath by now?

WHITCHURCH (*brazenly*) Bath? Julia's out with the other girls.

MR PECK. But I thought you said she was having a bath. It did seem rather peculiar, for Julia.

WHITCHURCH. At this time of day? (*With a forced laugh and tapping Mr Peck on his chest*) Now, I'm afraid someone else is rambling, Mr. Peck. (*Briskly*) Come along, I'll show you the classroom accommodation. Come along, Mr Peck—Mrs Peck. (*She leads the way firmly to the doors up* R)

(*The* PECKS *move up* R)

MRS PECK. Perhaps we could have a little peep at Julia's woodwork.

WHITCHURCH (*turning*) Her what?

MRS PECK. In the carpenter's shop. She wrote that she's been doing the most interesting things with a chisel.

WHITCHURCH. Yes, I've put a stop to that.

MR PECK. Put a stop to it?

WHITCHURCH. Er—yes. She's done quite enough chiselling for one term.

(MISS WHITCHURCH *and the* PECKS *exit up* R. MR PECK *closes the doors behind them*)

MR SOWTER (*off; calling*) Pond.

(MR SOWTER *enters aggressively through the french windows. He is a short, pugnacious, self-important man of middle age, soberly dressed. He wears an "Anthony Eden" hat and carries gloves. He is followed by* MRS SOWTER, *who is tall, stately and severe*)

(*As he enters*) Pond! (*He moves* LC) What the devil's happened to the feller? Does he think we're going to wait all afternoon?

MRS SOWTER (*moving above the table* C) Ridiculous.

MR SOWTER. That's putting it mildly. If this is a sample of the school's efficiency, we're wasting Cyril's time and our money. Rudeness and procrastination, that's about all the boy's likely to learn here. (*He eases down* L) He might just as well be at home——

MRS SOWTER. Edgar!

MR SOWTER (*turning impatiently*) You know well enough what I mean. (*He looks around*) Common room, I suppose. Flowers—cushions—don't like the look of it.

MRS SOWTER (*looking around*) Effeminate.

MR SOWTER (*moving to the door down* L, *opening it and calling*) Pond.

(MRS SOWTER *sees the needlework on the table* C, *moves down* L *of the table, picks up the pyjamas and eyes them with asperity*)

(*He closes the door and turns*) Not there. (*He sees the pyjamas*) Great Scott! What in the name of thunder . . .?

MRS SOWTER. Pyjamas.

MR SOWTER (*easing* LC) I know that. But look at them—damn it—they've got frills. What's a thing like that doing in a school like this?

MRS SOWTER (*replacing the pyjamas*) Inexplicable. (*She moves down* R)

MR SOWTER. We'll see about that. (*He moves to the french windows and calls*) Pond! (*He crosses to the doors up* R) Oh, roast the feller. (*He opens the doors up* R *and calls*) Pond. (*He turns and moves* LC) Ask me, we've been led up the garden—sending the boy here. Worse than the other place. Not a soul about. (*He points through the french windows*) Fine afternoon—not even a game being played.

MRS SOWTER. Incomprehensible.

MR SOWTER. Certainly is. (*He moves to the downstage* L *corner of the table* C) As for that so-called waiting-room—confounded impertinence.

MRS SOWTER. What?

MR SOWTER. Didn't you see it? (*He moves to Mrs Sowter and indicates an imaginary notice board*) Notice on the wall—"In front of the children, kindly moderate your language." Of all the bl——

MRS SOWTER (*sharply*) Edgar!

(JOYCE *enters through the french windows*)

JOYCE (*crossing to Mrs Sowter; confidently*) Good afternoon. (*She holds out her hand*)

(MR *and* MRS SOWTER *stare at her in surprise.* MR SOWTER *removes his hat*)

(*With a smile, shaking Mrs Sowter's hand*) I don't think we've met before. I only joined the staff last term.

MR SOWTER (*crossing* L *below the table* C; *horrified*) The staff! (*To Mrs Sowter*) What did I tell you? Led up the garden.

MRS SOWTER (*reflectively*) Matron?

MR SOWTER. Matron? She doesn't look like one. (*To Joyce*) Are you?

JOYCE (*moving below the table* C) No, I'm one of the mistresses.

MR SOWTER (*aghast*) One of them. (*To Mrs Sowter*) D'you hear that? (*He moves to the table* C, *puts his hat and gloves on it and holds up the pyjamas accusingly to Joyce*) These are yours, I suppose?

JOYCE (*looking at Mr Sowter curiously*) That's the Lower Third's fancy needlework. Quite good, isn't it, for juniors?

MR SOWTER (*beside himself*) Fancy needlework! You mean they make these darn things?

JOYCE. All sorts of things—tea-cosies, night-gowns——

MR SOWTER (*choking*) Night-gowns? (*He drops the pyjamas on the table* C *and turns to Mrs Sowter*) You see where your choice has landed us? *Night-gowns!* (*He turns to Joyce*) Our boy's in the Lower Third—if he *is* still a boy——

JOYCE (*dismayed*) You aren't Mr and Mrs Peck?

MR SOWTER (*aggressively*) Peck? Why should we be?

MRS SOWTER (*frigidly*) Sowter.

MR SOWTER (*to Joyce; grimly*) And the sooner I see Pond the better. (*He moves above the table* C) He gave us his solemn promise—in writing—(*he bangs on the table* C *to emphasize his words*) that he and his staff were bachelors, and he wouldn't have a mistress in the place.

JOYCE (*moving* L *of Mr Sowter*) Well—you see—I'm not really a mistress—I'm—I'm actually his niece. I'm helping out during the staff shortage.

MR SOWTER (*disbelievingly*) And the others are all relations, too, I suppose?

JOYCE. Yes—that's right.

MR SOWTER. I see. (*He looks straight at her*) Well, you'd better go and fetch your—uncle.

JOYCE. I think I had. (*She moves to the door down* L) Would you mind waiting in the study? (*She opens the door*)

MR SOWTER (*rudely*) Yes, I would. We've had enough of waiting-rooms.

MRS SOWTER (*crossing to the door down* L) Edgar——

MR SOWTER (*resignedly*) Oh, very well. (*He picks up his hat and gloves and moves down* L)

(MR *and* MRS SOWTER *exit down* L. JOYCE *closes the door.*
    As she turns, MISS WHITCHURCH *enters agitatedly up* R, *leaving the doors open*)

JOYCE (*moving* LC; *urgently*) Where's Mr Pond?

WHITCHURCH (*moving* R *of Joyce*) Never mind that. Where are Miss Gossage and the girls?

JOYCE. You sent them down to the baths.

WHITCHURCH (*impatiently*) That's been countermanded long ago. Didn't Barbara tell you? The Pecks are here.

JOYCE (*nodding*) So are the Sowters. (*She indicates the door down* L) They're in there.

WHITCHURCH (*horrified*) What?

JOYCE. They want Mr Pond.

WHITCHURCH. Well, they can't have him. I've got the Pecks in the library, and if they don't see Julia soon, I don't know what might happen. (*She leads* JOYCE *by the hand to the french windows*) Go down to the baths and hurry them. No. (*She stops and brings* JOYCE *back to* LC) You'd better stay here and keep an eye on the study. (*Perplexed*) I daren't leave the Pecks—— (*She turns towards the doors up* R)

(*As she does so,* HOPCROFT, *reading a boys' magazine, passes the doors on his way upstairs*)

(*She runs and grabs Hopcroft's arm. Hurriedly*) Er—boy— Hopcroft, or whatever your name is. (*She pulls him into the room* R *of the table* C) Come in here.

HOPCROFT (*a look of disarming innocence on his face*) I don't know anything about it, Miss Whitchurch.

WHITCHURCH. About what? (*Before he can answer*) Never mind—— (*She snatches the magazine out of his hand and throws it on the table* C) Go down to the baths and tell Miss Gossage and the girls to hurry up to the playing field.

HOPCROFT (*swallowing*) I can't do that, Miss Whitchurch.

WHITCHURCH. *Can't.* I'm telling you to.

HOPCROFT. I mean—*they* can't.

WHITCHURCH. Oh, and why not?

HOPCROFT. They haven't got any clothes.

WHITCHURCH. No clothes?

JOYCE. What d'you mean?

HOPCROFT. They've been pinch . . . taken away.

WHITCHURCH (*in an awful voice*) Hopcroft——

HOPCROFT. I didn't do it—I can swear to that.

WHITCHURCH (*ominously*) Someone's going to pay for this.

HOPCROFT (*turning away a little* R; *involuntarily*) Half a crown.

WHITCHURCH (*sharply*) What?

HOPCROFT (*hastily*) Nothing, Miss Whitchurch.

JOYCE (*to Miss Whitchurch*) I'd better get some things and he can take them down.

WHITCHURCH. Do.

(JOYCE *and* HOPCROFT *moves to the doors up* R)

(*She thinks of something*) No—wait. (*She moves and grabs* JOYCE'S *arm, pulls her to the door down* L, *remembers the Sowters are there, and pulling her* LC, *speaks in an undertone*) He can't go into the baths.

JOYCE. They're not locked in, are they?

WHITCHURCH (*still in an undertone*) It's not locks I'm thinking of. (*Still more quietly*) They've got no clothes on. (*She resumes her normal tones*) He'll have to throw the things over the wall——

JOYCE. With a note saying "Put them on and come up here at once."

WHITCHURCH. You get the clothes while I write the note——

(JOYCE *and* MISS WHITCHURCH *move quickly to the doors up* R)

JOYCE. Better mark it "urgent".

WHITCHURCH (*grabbing Hopcroft's arm*) Come along, Hopcroft. No time to lose. Best foot forward.

(JOYCE, MISS WHITCHURCH *and* HOPCROFT *exit up* R, *leaving the doors open, and go hurriedly up the stairs.*
As they do so, MR SOWTER *enters down* L)

MR SOWTER (*calling*) Pond! (*He waits a moment*) Blast the feller! (*He speaks off*) No sign of him yet——

(MR SOWTER *exits down* L, *closing the door.* MR *and* MRS PECK, *looking very worried, enter up* R. MR PECK *closes the doors*)

MRS PECK (*moving* R *of the table* C) Well, really, it all seems very queer, dear.

MR PECK (*setting the chair* R *of the table* C *for Mrs Peck*) I want to sit down.

MRS PECK (*seating herself in the chair* R *of the table* C) No Julia. Miss Whitchurch decidedly not herself.

MR PECK (*sitting in the easy chair* R) Mrs Pond, you mean.

MRS PECK. That's another thing—married for fifteen years and never mentioned it.

MR PECK (*leaning back in the chair*) Such things are not for us to question—after all, marriages are made in heaven——

MRS PECK (*idly glancing at the letters on the table*) Yes, dear, but this one was in Australia.

(RAINBOW, *muttering resentfully and carrying a netball goal-post, passes from* R *to* L *across the outside of the french windows*)

(*She sees a particular letter on the table and picks it up*) Well, what a surprise, right in front of my eyes. A letter from Julia.

MR PECK (*sitting up*) Left here for the post, presumably.

MRS PECK (*rising*) It's not even stuck down. (*She opens the letter and eases down* R *of the table* C)

MR PECK. D'you think you should? (*He rises and moves* R *of Mrs Peck*)

MRS PECK. Well, it's addressed to us. (*She reads the letter delightedly*) "Went for a nature study ramble this morning." (*She suddenly thinks of something and looks puzzled*) How can she have written that when she's not back from it yet?

(MR *and* MRS PECK *look at one another.* MR SOWTER, *followed by* MRS SOWTER, *enters angrily down* L)

MR SOWTER (*moving* LC) Look here—I haven't got all afternoon—— (*He sees the Pecks*) Huh! (*He turns to Mrs Sowter*) More of the staff, I suppose?

MR PECK. Er—no. We're parents.

MR SOWTER. Oh. So are we.

MRS SOWTER. Yes.

MRS PECK. Really? (*She crosses to Mrs Sowter*) My husband and I were just saying, we're rather worried about conditions here——

MR SOWTER. I'm not surprised.

MRS SOWTER. Disgraceful.

MR PECK. Well, I wouldn't put it as strongly as that——

MR SOWTER. Wouldn't you? What about the fancy needlework. (*He moves to the table* C) Have you seen these? (*He snatches up something from the work-basket and holds it up. It turns out to be the lace-edged knickers. He stares at them*) Good God! It's worse than I thought.

(MRS SOWTER *crosses Mrs Peck, takes the knickers from* MR SOWTER *and puts them back into the basket*)

MRS PECK. Well, that sort of thing comes in very useful, you know——

MRS SOWTER (*outraged*) Useful?

MRS PECK (*nodding*) When they're grown up.

MR SOWTER (*choking*) When they're . . .

MR PECK (*crossing to* R *of Mrs Peck*) What we feel more concerned about is our daughter's mental and physical well-being——

MR SOWTER. Your daughter's? What's that got to do with it?

(MISS WHITCHURCH *enters up* R, *leaving the door open. She starts in horror as she sees the Sowters and Pecks together, hurriedly crosses below the table, and stands between them*)

WHITCHURCH. I'm sorry, but I can't have two lots of parents in here at the same time. It's—er—it's against the rules.

MR SOWTER (*to Mrs Sowter*) Another of 'em.

MRS SOWTER (*looking at Miss Whitchurch*) Fantastic.

WHITCHURCH (*with umbrage*) I beg your pardon?

MR SOWTER (*to Miss Whitchurch*) I want to see Pond.

WHITCHURCH (*with asperity*) Mr Pond is otherwise engaged.

MRS PECK (*to Miss Whitchurch*) Mrs Pond—there's something I don't understand.

MR SOWTER. *Mrs Pond?* You must be his mother.

WHITCHURCH (*livid*) I am nothing of the kind!

MR PECK. It was a surprise to us, too—we'd no idea they were married.

MRS SOWTER. Married!

MR SOWTER (*turning to Mrs Sowter*) This is the last straw! It was bad enough when I found out he kept women here.

(*The* PECKS *stare in astonishment*)

WHITCHURCH (*to the Pecks; hurriedly*) If you wouldn't mind waiting in the study—— (*She ushers the Pecks to the door down* L *and opens it*)

MRS PECK. But there's something I must ask about Julia——

WHITCHURCH (*firmly*) Julia later—please.

(*The* PECKS *exit reluctantly down* L. MISS WHITCHURCH *closes the door*)

MR SOWTER (*suspiciously*) Julia? Who's she?

WHITCHURCH. Er—the school mascot. She's—er—she's a nanny-goat. Now, Mr Sowter, if you wouldn't mind, there's a waiting-room just along the . . . (*She pushes him below the table* C)

MR SOWTER (*furiously*) Another waiting-room?

(JOYCE *enters hurriedly through the french windows*)

JOYCE (*moving down* L *of Miss Whitchurch*) It's all right—he's taken them down——

WHITCHURCH (*hurriedly*) Quite, quite, Miss Harper—— (*To the Sowters. Blandly*) This is a cousin of mine——

MRS SOWTER. Cousin?

MR SOWTER. I thought she was your niece by marriage.

JOYCE (*hastily*) I—er—I'm Pond's niece by his first wife.

MR SOWTER (*to Mrs Sowter*) Niece by his first wife? Sounds illegal to me.

(BARBARA *enters agitatedly and hurriedly through the french windows, and runs down between Miss Whitchurch and Joyce*)

BARBARA (*breathlessly*) Miss Whitchurch—I was down by the baths—and I just saw one of the boys—with a whole lot of . . .

WHITCHURCH (*severely*) Barbara. Don't tell stories.

MR SOWTER (*ominously*) Another of Pond's nieces, I suppose?

WHITCHURCH. Barbara is one of my little girls—nothing whatever to do with Mr Pond.

(JOYCE *sits in the easy chair* L)

BARBARA (*to the Sowters*) How d'you do? I'm Barbara Cahoun —*not* spelt Colquhoun.

MR SOWTER (*to Mrs Sowter; puzzled*) A Cahoun?

BARBARA (*persistently*) Miss Whitchurch——

WHITCHURCH (*angrily*) Barbara—that will do. (*She pinches Barbara's arm*)

BARBARA. Ow! (*In amazed reproach*) Miss Whitchurch!

WHITCHURCH (*to the Sowters*) She hasn't got used to my married name yet.

MR SOWTER (*bewildered*) Yes, but if she's your little girl and her name's Cahoun, and you were Miss Whitchurch before you married Pond, she must be a little . . .

MRS SOWTER. Edgar!

MR SOWTER (*angrily*) There's something fishy going on here——

BARBARA. There's something fishy down at the baths——

WHITCHURCH (*severely*) Barbara!

MR SOWTER. Oh yes, there is. And I want to see Pond—— (*He crosses to the fireplace*)

(MR *and* MRS PECK *enter down* L. MRS PECK *is still holding the letter.* JOYCE *rises.* BARBARA *eases to* L *of* JOYCE)

MR PECK (*with an air of determination*) Miss Whitchurch—my wife and I have been talking, and we demand—yes, demand—to see Julia at once.

MRS PECK (*indicating the letter*) There's something very peculiar going on——

MR SOWTER (*to Mrs Sowter*) That's just what *I* said.

MR PECK. What have you done with Julia?

MR SOWTER. Never mind about the blessed goat! I want to see Pond.

MR PECK (*storming across to Mr Sowter with his fist clenched and arm raised; outraged*) You—you call my daughter a goat, sir!

(MRS PECK *follows Mr Peck across.* RAINBOW *enters up* R, *leaving the doors open. He is about to cross to the french windows but is arrested by the argument and stands watching*)

MR SOWTER. I never mentioned your daughter.

(JOYCE *and* BARBARA *ease down* L)

MR PECK. Oh yes, you did.

MR SOWTER (*shouting*) I did not.

(MRS SOWTER *crosses above the table* C *and then down to support Mr Sowter, standing on his left. The* PECKS *and* SOWTERS *make a group in front of the fireplace. As all speak simultaneously, their words are indecipherable*)

WHITCHURCH (*below the* L *corner of the table* C; *agitatedly above the uproar*) Rainbow—Rainbow——

RAINBOW (*bitterly*) If I've got to change them ruddy contraptions again—— (*He eases above the table* C)

(HOPCROFT *enters agitatedly through the french windows and runs down* L *of Miss Whitchurch*)

HOPCROFT. Miss Whitchurch! Miss Harper!

(*The* SOWTERS *and* PECKS *break off from quarrelling, turn and look at Hopcroft*)

They're coming up the drive.

JOYCE. Who's coming up the drive?

HOPCROFT. Miss Gossage and the girls.

MR SOWTER (*outraged*) *Gossage and the girls?*

MRS PECK. Does that include Julia?

WHITCHURCH. Certainly. The whole school. (*With sudden terrible misgiving*) Then who have we sent those clothes to—down at the baths?

(HOPCROFT *moves up stage to* L *of Rainbow*)

RAINBOW. Who d'you think it is?

(RAINBOW *and* HOPCROFT *start arguing*)

WHITCHURCH. Silence, Rainbow.

MRS PECK (*indicating the letter*) I still don't understand——

(MISS GOSSAGE *enters up* R *and moves to* R *of Miss Whitchurch*)

MRS SOWTER (*angrily*) Silence!

MR PECK (*furiously*) How dare you address my wife . . .

MR SOWTER. *I want to see Pond.*

(*All these last speeches are almost simultaneous. As the row is at its height,* BILLINGS, POND *and* TASSELL *enter through the french windows. They arrive running, and are dressed as schoolgirls, in gym frocks, panama hats and white socks.* POND *has a broad pale blue sash down across his chest with "CAPTAIN" embroidered on it in puce. As they get* L *of the table* C, *they realize the presence of the parents.*

In consternation, they dither, then turn, dash for the door down L *and exit,* TASSELL *first, then* POND *and lastly* BILLINGS. *The* SOWTERS *and* PECKS *stare aghast.* RAINBOW *and* HOPCROFT *watch amazed.* JOYCE *covers her eyes. As* TASSELL *reaches the door down* L, MISS WHITCHURCH *faints into* GOSSAGE's *arms*)

CURTAIN

ACT III

SCENE—*The same. Two hours later.*

When the CURTAIN *rises, the table has been cleared and re-set with the three dining chairs in the Act I position. The vase of flowers has gone from the mantelpiece and the waste-paper basket has been emptied.* MISS WHITCHURCH *is seated on the stool down* R *speaking on the telephone. Her manner is exasperated in the extreme.* MISS GOSSAGE *stands at Miss Whitchurch's left elbow, holding a Ministry memo.*

WHITCHURCH (*speaking into the telephone*) Hullo, Hul*lo.* Ministry of Devacuation? . . . I must have . . . (*She pauses*)

(MISS GOSSAGE *indicates a name on the memo*)

(*She reads, speaking into the telephone*) Mr Fraphampton's home address . . . (*Angrily*) What do you mean, you thought I'd got it? (*To Miss Gossage*) He says I must have got it. (*Into the telephone*) Don't be ridiculous . . . Hullo. *Hullo.* Give me Mr—— (*she consults the memo again*) Fraphampton's secretary . . . You thought what? . . .

(BILLINGS, *dressed in sports coat and grey flannels, enters up* R. *He is dusty and very hot. He closes the door behind him, moves to his locker below the fireplace, reaches over Miss Whitchurch, and opens the locker*)

If I *were* his secretary, would I be asking for her? . . . Oh, this is hopeless. I suppose that *is* the Ministry of Devac . . . I am *not.* I'm speaking to them.

(BILLINGS *takes his scarf from the locker. It brushes across the telephone*)

(*She brushes the scarf angrily aside*) *Will* you get off my line. (*She flashes the receiver rest*) What is all this? Hullo, hul*lo.* Exchange! Exchange!

(POND *enters agitatedly down* L, *mopping his face with his handkerchief. He is dressed in his academic attire*)

POND (*moving to the chair* L *of the table* C; *to Billings*) Found anything? (*He sits*)

BILLINGS (*exhaustedly*) Not even a cowshed. (*He moves to the chair* R *of the table* C, *sits and mops his face with the scarf*)

WHITCHURCH (*into the telephone; exasperatedly*) Exchange! Exchange! (*She lifts the instrument off the table and puts it on her knees*)

GOSSAGE (*turning and smiling sympathetically at Billings*) Nothing vacant? (*She moves* R *of Billings*)

BILLINGS (*bitterly*) Apart from the faces of the population—no.

72

(MISS GOSSAGE *moves to the fireplace and stands with her back to it*)

WHITCHURCH (*into the telephone; angrily*) What do you mean, number please? I'm through to a number . . . (*She flashes the receiver rest repeatedly*)

POND (*to Billings*) I've been trying to telephone the Ministry. All I could get was some fool of a female saying (*he imitates Miss Whitchurch's tone*) "Hullo, hul*lo*." So in the end I——

WHITCHURCH (*into the telephone*) Hullo, hul*lo*.

(POND *and* BILLINGS *react and rise.* BILLINGS *puts the scarf on the table* C)

POND. Eh?

(POND *and* BILLINGS *stare at Miss Whitchurch*)

WHITCHURCH (*into the telephone*) I tell you I was speaking to London, but some mentally deficient numbskull of a man was on my line.

(POND *reacts*)

Will you tell me what I can do? (*Her tone changes. Very severely*) For that vulgarity I shall report you to the supervisor. Give me the super . . .

BILLINGS (*moving to Miss Whitchurch*) I shouldn't bother.

POND (*to Miss Whitchurch*) I should have told you. That telephone's a party line to the one in my study.

(MISS WHITCHURCH *replaces the receiver, lifts the instrument off her knees, and still holding it, rises*)

WHITCHURCH. You mean—I've been wasting my time talking to *you*? (*She moves towards Pond, but is brought up with a jerk as the limit of the telephone cord is reached. The instrument is nearly jerked out of her hand*)

(BILLINGS *takes the instrument from her and replaces it on the table down* R)

POND (*with umbrage*) And vice versa.

GOSSAGE. If you ask me, it's utterly imposs. How *can* we produce another set of premises by six o'clock?

BILLINGS. On a Saturday, too, when even the nearest agents are half-day, as well as half-dead.

WHITCHURCH (*moving to the telephone*) I'd better try again.

BILLINGS. You haven't a hope, you know.

WHITCHURCH (*lifting the receiver*) Never say die. (*She speaks into the telephone*) Hullo, hul*lo*.

POND (*impatiently*) Let me. (*He crosses to* R *of Miss Whitchurch and forcibly takes the receiver from her. He turns clockwise to face the audience, so that the receiver cord is across his chest*)

(BILLINGS, R *of Pond, and* MISS WHITCHURCH *with* MISS GOSSAGE L *of her, crowd round watching anxiously. They all lift the cord over Pond's head to disentangle him*)

(*He dials once and speaks into the telephone with abject politeness*) Oh, good afternoon. I—I wonder if I could possibly trouble you to secure me a number? It's rather a long way off, I'm afraid . . . You can? Oh, splendid. (*He sits on the stool, beams and nods at the others*)

WHITCHURCH (*contemptuously*) Groveller.

POND (*into the telephone*) I want Whitehall one-double-one-one-one. Yes. This is Little Upton O—two . . . (*Louder*) O-two—O for nought and T for two . . . Oh, that's very good of you. Thank you. (*He replaces the receiver. Jubilantly*) They're going to ring me back. (*He rises*)

(TASSELL *and* JOYCE *enter companionably through the french windows.* TASSELL *is now wearing sports coat and grey flannels.* JOYCE *is wearing the same dress as in Act II.* POND, MISS GOSSAGE *and* MISS WHITCHURCH *turn expectantly*)

BILLINGS (*crossing below the table* C) Well, it's quite obvious *they* haven't found anything.

(MISS WHITCHURCH *moves to the chair* R *of the table* C *and sits*)

TASSELL. How did you guess?

BILLINGS. If *I* couldn't, with my mind on the job. (*He sits in the chair* L *of the table* C)

TASSELL (*glaring at Billings*) Now listen, if you're suggesting . . .

POND (*moving above the table* C) Oh, come now, this is no time for squabbling and chiff-chaff.

GOSSAGE (*moving* R *of Pond and trying to be helpful*) The chiff-chaff is a bird, I think.

POND (*sitting in the chair above the table* C; *irritably*) Well, chitter-chatter, then.

(MISS GOSSAGE *sits in the chair by the bookcase*)

WHITCHURCH. Mr Pond's quite right. Now's the time for team-work. Two heads are better than one——

BILLINGS. Not in this establishment.

(MISS WHITCHURCH *glares at Billings*)

JOYCE (*to Miss Whitchurch*) What did Mr Peck say exactly?

WHITCHURCH. Unless we can find somewhere else by six o'clock, he'll feel morally obliged to withdraw his daughter and inform all the other parents of his reasons for so doing.

(JOYCE *sits in the easy chair* L)

TASSELL (*to Pond*) And the Sowters said the same thing to you? (*He perches himself on the upstage arm of the easy chair* L)

Pond. Not in so many words.
Billings. I can believe that.
Joyce. They must know we can't possibly do it.
Whitchurch. The Pecks are already packing Julia's things.
Billings. We might just as well start packing ours.
Pond. Oh, that it should come to this!

(*The telephone bell rings*)

(*Excitedly*) That'll be the Ministry.

(*Everybody rises suddenly.* Miss Whitchurch, Pond, Billings *and* Tassell *make a concerted dash for the telephone.* Tassell *gets there first and lifts the receiver.* Joyce *and* Miss Gossage *cross above the table* c *and join the group*)

Tassell (*into the telephone*) Hullo, is that the Ministry of Devacuation? . . . I'd like to talk to . . .

(Billings *wrenches the receiver from* Tassell)

Billings (*into the telephone*) Hullo, is that the Ministry of Whatever-it-is?

(Miss Whitchurch *irritably grabs the receiver from Billings*)

Whitchurch (*into the telephone*) Hullo, hul*lo*. St Swithins here —I'd like to speak to . . .

(Pond *seizes the receiver*)

Oh, you are so rude——
Pond (*into the telephone*) Hullo, hul*lo*. (*He reacts at having involuntarily copied Miss Whitchurch*) This is Hilary Hall . . . Said what just now? . . . (*Exasperatedly*) Oh, very well then—St Hithins and Swilary Hall . . . Yes, yes . . . What? . . .
Whitchurch (*at Pond's elbow*) Speak to them severely.
Tassell (*at Pond's other elbow*) Tell them it's life and death.
Gossage (*loudly*) Pitch it hot and strong——
Pond (*into the telephone; agitatedly*) I can't hear you . . .

(Miss Whitchurch, Tassell *and* Miss Gossage *think he is speaking to them*)

Whitchurch ⎫
Tassell   ⎬ (*together; loudly*) ⎰ Speak to them severely.
Gossage ⎭   ⎱ Tell them it's life and death.
                                   Pitch it hot and strong——
Pond (*furiously*) Silence, boys—I mean—everyone—— (*He turns round to the group, and again gets entangled in the cord*)

(*The others disentangle Pond and the uproar subsides*)

(*Into the telephone*) Hullo . . . What I said was . . . You said what? . . . Eh? Oh, oh, oh. (*He replaces the receiver. In a voice of doom*) Closed till Monday.

ALL. Oh.

(*There is general despair.* TASSELL *moves to the bookcase and leans against it.* RAINBOW *enters through the french windows*)

RAINBOW (*to Pond*) Beg pardon, sir. (*He moves down* L *of the table* C)

POND (*moving below the table* C; *irritably*) Oh, whatever is it, Rainbow? What is it?

RAINBOW. I only wanted to be suggestive.

(*All stare at him*)

WHITCHURCH (*moving* R *of the table* C; *to Miss Gossage*) I knew his glands wanted seeing to.

POND (*to Rainbow; hurriedly*) Thank you, Rainbow, not now.

RAINBOW. You don't want to hear it, then?

BILLINGS. If it's one of those limericks—certainly not.

RAINBOW (*shrugging his shoulders*) I only thought they might do —for temporary housing, so to speak. (*He turns to the french windows*)

(POND *moves* LC)

TASSELL. Housing? (*He grabs Rainbow and pushes him below the table* C, R *of Pond*)

(JOYCE *runs across to* L)

BILLINGS			You haven't found something?
POND			Oh, incredible!
GOSSAGE	}	(*together*) {	You wizard man!
WHITCHURCH			What is it?
JOYCE			Where is it?

(*They all crowd round Rainbow,* MISS WHITCHURCH, MISS GOSSAGE *and* BILLINGS R *of him,* POND, TASSELL *and* JOYCE L *of him*)

RAINBOW. In the field at the back of the halt. Three L.M.S. railway carriages.

WHITCHURCH (*aghast*) Rolling stock!

POND. Oh, but that's going a bit far, surely.

RAINBOW. They aren't going anywhere. They're disused railway carriages.

WHITCHURCH (*scornfully*) Three. For an entire school.

RAINBOW (*defensively*) There's eight compartments to a carriage. (*He takes a scrap of paper and a stub of pencil from his pocket and works it out as he speaks*) Four a side in each. That's sixty-four. Three carriages. A hundred and ninety-two in all.

BILLINGS (*to Tassell*) We could do with him on the teaching staff here.

RAINBOW. Sleep one on each rack, and one on the seat, and there's still room for ninety-six.

TASSELL (*warming to the idea*) True enough. Knock off one carriage for classrooms——

RAINBOW. The guard's van for the staff.

JOYCE (*breaking down* L) And you've still got room for over sixty.

(TASSELL *joins Joyce down* L)

POND (*enthusiastically*) By Jove! So you have.

WHITCHURCH (*also warming to the idea*) First class for the senior school——

POND. Third for the juniors.

GOSSAGE (*moving to the fireplace*) Plenty of good healthy fresh air——

TASSELL. And every modern convenience . . .

BILLINGS. At each end of the corridor. (*He turns and moves up* R)

(JOYCE *sits in the easy chair* L. TASSELL *perches himself on the upstage arm of it*)

POND (*weightily*) I doubt if we'll do better. (*He sits in the chair* L *of the table* C)

WHITCHURCH (*sitting in the chair* R *of the table* C) Rainbow, I congratulate you. (*She leans forward and shakes Rainbow's hand*)

POND (*warmly*) Hear, hear.

RAINBOW (*moving round the* L *end above the table* C) Mind you, they are being used for poultry, but if I know Jim Potter, you see him all right, and he'll soon turn his chicks out.

BILLINGS (*moving down* R; *to Miss Whitchurch*) And then you can turn your chicks in.

WHITCHURCH (*turning and looking at Billings; sharply*) Yours, you mean.

POND (*rising*) You don't expect us to vacate our own premises?

WHITCHURCH (*rising and moving below the table* C) You don't expect us to sleep in railway carriages with laying hens?

POND. After all, L.M.S. *Was* a very good line, you know.

WHITCHURCH (*with great asperity*) Quite apart from any question of courtesy, do you think for one moment that the Pecks would agree to it? Think of Julia—a delicate child—living in a railway carriage.

BILLINGS. You could always put her in a non-smoker.

POND (*gloomy again*) I'd forgotten the parents.

JOYCE (*nodding*) If our Pecks would object, so would your Sowters, from what I know of them.

(*The others nod gloomily*)

WHITCHURCH (*looking at Rainbow; irritably*) Idiotic suggestion, Rainbow. (*She sits again in the chair* R *of the table* C)

(RAINBOW *bridles, annoyed*)

POND (*hastily*) Never mind, Rainbow. You meant it for the best, I'm sure. (*He sits again in the chair L of the table C*)

RAINBOW (*moving to the doors up R; defensively*) I still think it was feasible.

BILLINGS. Hopeless.

(RAINBOW *exits up R, closing the doors behind him.* BILLINGS *eases up R*)

TASSELL (*rising and moving above the table C*) As far as I can see, there's only one hope left, and that's bribery.

WHITCHURCH (*stiffly*) Bribery? Of whom?

TASSELL. The packing parents upstairs. Dangle a little something in front of them to make them change their minds—or give us a few weeks' grace, anyway.

POND. Quite impracticable. The Sowters are rolling in money.

GOSSAGE. And the Pecks wouldn't look at it.

JOYCE. But money isn't the only thing. If we could only convince them that the children are doing better here than they would anywhere else—I mean, top of the class, and so on——

WHITCHURCH. Julia's been in the bottom class ever since she joined us, and nearly always bottom of that. (*She brightens a little*) Of course, that does leave all the more scope for promotion.

GOSSAGE (*eagerly*) There's games, too.

(TASSELL *moves to L of Pond*)

POND (*enthusiastically*) Games. The Sowters would jump at that. (*To Tassell*) Suppose you put little Cyril in the first eleven?

TASSELL (*grimly*) Half an hour, and there'd only be ten.

GOSSAGE (*looking at her watch*) Whatever we do, we'll have to pull our socks up. It's a quarter to six now. Their train goes at half past.

POND (*nodding*) The last one, what's more.

BILLINGS (*suddenly*) We're mad—all of us! (*He moves above the table C*)

(*All protest*)

No, no—it's the obvious thing——

(*As he speaks,* HOPCROFT *enters up R, closing the doors behind him. He is carrying a piece of paper. All are looking eagerly at Billings*)

POND (*impatiently*) Come, come, what is it then?

HOPCROFT (*thinking the question was directed at him*) Please sir, Matron asked me to . . .

POND (*irritably*) Not you, Hopcroft. Wait a minute. Yes, Billings?

BILLINGS. It's simple. Don't let them catch the last train. If we can only see they miss it—there are no trains on Sunday. Every-where's full up, and they'll have to stay here. That means they won't do anything till Monday.

TASSELL. And in the meantime, we can really go to work on them.

GOSSAGE (*excitedly*) A whole lot can happen in the next forty-eight hours.

BILLINGS. I should imagine so—judging by the last four.

WHITCHURCH (*to Miss Gossage*) I might let Mr Peck preach the sermon tomorrow—as a compensation for missing his train.

POND. Sowter can see the boys doing their early morning jerks——

TASSELL. And having cold showers.

JOYCE (*surprised*) Do they on Sundays?

TASSELL. They don't on week-days, but it's never too late to start.

(JOYCE *rises, moves outside the french windows and stands looking at the view.* BILLINGS *picks up his scarf from the table*)

POND (*rising and easing above the* L *end of the table* C) I'd better start delaying action straight away.

WHITCHURCH (*rising and moving above Miss Gossage*) I'll see to the Pecks.

POND (*pausing as he thinks of something*) Wait a minute—what if they want a taxi ordered?

BILLINGS. Tell 'em you'll see to it—then don't.

POND (*horrified*) Go back on my own word? (*Cheerfully*) Good idea. (*He crosses to the doors up* R *and sees Hopcroft*) What are you doing here?

HOPCROFT (*slightly aggrieved*) You told me to wait, sir.

POND. Oh, did I? Well, what is it?

HOPCROFT (*handing Pond the note*) From Mrs Hampstead, sir.

POND (*unfolding the note and reading it*) "From Matron. Kindly send someone. I wish to leave the room."

WHITCHURCH (*stiffly*) Well, really——

POND (*to Billings and Tassell*) Oh, my goodness. I left her in charge of the boys, while we busied ourselves with the emergency.

TASSELL. That was over two hours ago.

BILLINGS. Now she's got an emergency of her own. (*He sits on the upstage edge of the table* C *with his back to the audience*)

POND (*agitatedly*) Yes, yes. Well, one of us will have to go and relieve her. (*To Hopcroft*) All right, Hopcroft.

(HOPCROFT *exits up* R, *leaving the door open*)

(*To Billings and Tassell*) See to it, will you, one of you.

(POND *exits up* R)

WHITCHURCH (*moving to the doors up* R) Where are the girls, Miss Gossage?

GOSSAGE (*moving* R *of Miss Whitchurch*) On the back lawn. I told them to snug down for an hour or two with Ruskin and Carlyle.
WHITCHURCH. In that case, they'd better have a high tea.

(MISS WHITCHURCH *and* MISS GOSSAGE *exit up* R, *closing the doors behind them*)

BILLINGS (*rising and moving to his locker below the fireplace*) If it's that whale steak again, they probably will. (*To* Tassell) Are you going to the relief of Hampstead, or am I?

(TASSELL *crosses quickly to Billings.* BILLINGS *puts his scarf in his locker and takes out a sheaf of papers*)

TASSELL (*glancing at Joyce; appealingly to Billings*) Look here, R.B.—it may be my last chance . . .
BILLINGS (*turning and leaving his locker door open*) But you've just been out for two hours with the damn girl——
TASSELL (*exasperatedly*) We were looking for school buildings.
BILLINGS (*staring at him; astonished*) Great Heavens! I believe you must have been. (*He stares at Tassell, shakes his head incredulously and moves to the door up* R)

(TASSELL *follows him anxiously*)

I know, I know.

(BILLINGS *exits up* R, *closing the door behind him.* TASSELL *moves below the table* C *as* JOYCE *turns and re-enters the room from outside the french windows.* TASSELL *holds out his arms to her as she moves down, but she goes straight past him to Billings' locker and closes it. As she then turns towards the doors up* R, *she is intercepted by* TASSELL *who moves quickly to the chair* R *of the table* C, *and puts the chair in Joyce's path to halt her*)

TASSELL (*as he swings the chair in front of her; sternly*) Miss Harper—

(JOYCE *stops and they gaze at each other across the chair*)

(*Tenderly*) Oh, Miss Harper—Dick—no, that's my name—Miss Harper—whatever happens now, it may be too late for anything to happen——

(BARBARA *enters through the french windows, moves to* L *of the table* C *and watches Tassell and Joyce*)

So what I'm trying to say is, if we separate, we shall have to part, so—so all afternoon—what I've wanted to say is——
BARBARA (*suddenly*) Oh, Miss Harper——
TASSELL (*vehemently*) Blast!
JOYCE (*to Tassell; innocently*) You wanted to say "Blast"?
TASSELL (*banging the chair* R *of the table* C *back into its original position; with feeling*) I wanted to say something very much worse than that.

JOYCE (*turning and moving down* RC) Yes, Barbara?

BARBARA (*moving below the* L *end of the table* C) Can I speak to you, Miss Harper? (*She looks meaningly at Tassell*) Alone. It's frightfully urgent.

(JOYCE *looks apologetically at Tassell*)

JOYCE. I say, do you mind awfully?

(TASSELL *glares at Barbara, then turns and exits up* R, *closing the doors behind him.* JOYCE *turns to Barbara enquiringly*)

BARBARA (*moving* C *below the table* C; *triumphantly*) It was miles easier than I thought.

JOYCE (*puzzled*) What was?

BARBARA. Getting rid of Mr Tassell.

JOYCE (*staring at her*) Do you mean to say . . .

BARBARA. I've noticed he's been pressing his unwelcome attentions on you for weeks now. And when you went off this afternoon —(*dramatically*) alone, in the secluded countryside . . .

JOYCE (*dryly*) What book have you been snugging down with on the lawn?

BARBARA (*innocently*) *Sartor Resartus* by Carlyle.

JOYCE. Never mind what you were told to read, what *were* you reading?

BARBARA (*swallowing*) *The Fruits of Passion.* I'm afraid it's not by Ruskin or Carlyle.

JOYCE. You'd better write out fifty times, "Fiction is nearly always stranger than truth", and give it me by lunch time tomorrow. (*She moves to the door up* R)

BARBARA (*protesting*) Oh, Miss Harper——

JOYCE (*stopping and turning*) Bring me that book, too.

BARBARA. But, Miss Harper——

JOYCE. And think yourself lucky I'm not giving you a misconduct mark for coming in here on false pretences.

(*Looking as severe as she can,* JOYCE *exits up* R, *closing the doors behind her.* BARBARA *stands for a moment in some dismay, then disconsolately moves up* R.

As she does so, HOPCROFT *appears at the french windows and peers in as if looking for someone. He sees Barbara and enters, moving down* LC)

HOPCROFT. Psst! I say, have you heard the news?

BARBARA (*moving down* RC; *delightedly*) Yes. Isn't it absolutely top score?

HOPCROFT (*surprised*) Top score?

BARBARA. Well, if the Pecks are going to spill the beans, we'll have to break up and go home. (*She leans on the table* C) I'm going to get my parents to engage Miss Harper as my private tutor.

HOPCROFT (*gloomily*) Don't be crackers. It's all off.

BARBARA (*dismayed*) Why? What's happened?

HOPCROFT. They're going to make them miss their train, and then go to work on them.

BARBARA (*mystified*) Who's going to work on who?

HOPCROFT. Your hags and our beaks are going to work on the Pecks and Sowters, to make them change their minds. (*He crosses Barbara to* R) We're going to have physical jerks all the week-end, while you listen to a sermon from old Peck.

BARBARA (*appalled*) Gosh! What a plate of tapioca!

HOPCROFT. If we could only make sure they catch the six-thirty somehow——

BARBARA. Anything I can do, count me in.

HOPCROFT (*delighted*) Shake.

(*There is the sound of voices off up* R)

BARBARA. Cave!

(BARBARA *and* HOPCROFT *hurry to the french windows and exit at a run as* POND *with* MR *and* MRS SOWTER *enter up* R. POND *opens the* L *door and* MR SOWTER *the* R. MRS SOWTER *enters between them and moves down* RC. POND *and* MR SOWTER *close their respective halves of the door*)

POND (*as they enter*) As I was saying, Mr Sowter—the most remarkable boy (*he moves down* R *of Mrs Sowter*) of his age I've ever had.

(MR SOWTER *moves to the fireplace*)

(*Impressively*) Do you know, Mr Tassell says he can't put him in the first eleven—it wouldn't be fair to the other ten.

MR SOWTER. Doesn't sound like Cyril

MRS SOWTER. Doesn't. (*She moves below the* L *end of the table* C)

POND (*moving* R *of Mrs Sowter; defensively*) Well, it's true—literally. The best bowler we've ever had. And that's after only a few hours' coaching. Think what two or three years would do.

MR SOWTER (*moving* R *of Pond; vehemently*) I know what two or three weeks have done. Prancing up here in a—a school-girl's what-d'you call it. (*In an outraged tone*) And if that's not enough, a form master whose name is Daisy.

(HOPCROFT *enters up* R, *closing the doors behind him*)

HOPCROFT (*moving down* R) Excuse me, sir——

POND (*irritably*) What is it? (*He crosses below Mr Sowter to Hopcroft*)

HOPCROFT. Excuse me, sir—but no-one's come to take prep. (*Very clearly—with a look at the Sowters*) And it's past six o'clock, sir.

POND (*quickly*) All right, Hopcroft—all right.

HOPCROFT (*persistently*) Quite a bit past six o'clock, sir.

MR SOWTER (*looking at his watch*) Yes, it is.

POND (*thoughtlessly*) Nonsense.

MRS SOWTER (*outraged*) Nonsense?

POND (*to Hopcroft; hastily*) I mean—nonsense. You won't miss the train—— (*To Mr Sowter. Agitatedly correcting himself*) I mean —run along and wait for prep. (*To Hopcroft. Desperately*) That will do, Hopcroft.

HOPCROFT. Yes, sir.

(HOPCROFT *exits up* R, *closing the doors behind him*)

POND (*crossing* L *below the Sowters; mopping his forehead*) Now, Mr Sowter, leave the young man with me, and I'm sure . . .

MR SOWTER (*firmly*) Mr Pond, have you or have you not dis-posed of that schoolful of women?

POND (*unhappily*) Well—not absolutely—but I have the highest hopes——

MRS SOWTER (*bluntly*) Luggage.

POND (*taken aback*) I beg your pardon?

MR SOWTER. We want the boy's luggage brought down.

POND (*agitatedly*) Oh, no, no, no.

MRS SOWTER (*formidably*) No?

POND (*intimidated*) No trouble at all.

(BILLINGS, *carrying his sheaf of papers, enters up* R *leaving the door open. He moves down* R)

(*He crosses below the Sowters to Billings, anxious for help*) Oh, Billings —Mr Sowter was just saying—his boy's bags ought to be taken down.

BILLINGS (*surprised, but pleased*) I entirely agree with him.

POND (*aghast*) What?

BILLINGS. Six of the best do him all the good in the world.

(*The* SOWTERS *glare at Billings*)

MR SOWTER (*angrily*) I'm asking for the boy's trunk to be dealt with.

BILLINGS. So am I.

MR SOWTER (*to Pond; impatiently*) Are you going to see to it, or must I?

(BILLINGS *stares at Mr Sowter, bewildered by the conversation*)

POND (*hastily*) No, no, not you. We'll attend to it. (*To Billings*) Er—Billings, ring for Rainbow, will you not (*he shakes his head*), and ask him to bring down Sowter's luggage.

BILLINGS (*enlightened*) Oh—luggage. (*He looks at Pond*) A bit early, isn't it?

MR SOWTER (*to Pond*) You ordered the taxi for six-fifteen, didn't you?

BILLINGS (*to Pond; interrupting*) Headmaster. (*To Mr Sowter*) Excuse me. (*He leads Pond aside to the fireplace and speaks apparently*

D*

confidentially, but making sure the Sowters can and do overhear) You're
not letting the Sowters go without showing them the mark?

POND (*confused*) Mark?

BILLINGS (*frowning at Pond*) On the pavilion. Where young
Sowter hit our best bowler for a sixer.

POND (*getting the idea*) Oh, that one.

MR SOWTER. I thought you said *Cyril* was your best bowler?

POND (*turning to Mr Sowter; thinking fast*) Our—er—best *googly*
bowler. (*He makes a "googly" bowling action*) But what a batsman!
(*Hurriedly*) Come, follow me—— (*He crosses below the Sowters to* LC)

MR SOWTER (*still dubious*) Hit a sixer into the pavilion? Cyril?
(*To Billings*) Is this some cock-and-bull story?

POND. No, no. Bat and ball. Come along, and I'll show you
while you're waiting.

(*The* SOWTERS *are reluctant*)

Please—I insist. Won't take five minutes. (*He hastily ushers the
Sowters to the french windows*)

MR SOWTER (*pausing and turning to Billings*) Look here, don't
forget to tell that porter to . . .

BILLINGS (*smiling disarmingly*) Don't worry, sir. I know just what
to tell the porter.

(POND *and* BILLINGS *exchange glances. The* SOWTERS *and* POND
exit through the french windows. BILLINGS *moves to his locker, puts his
papers on the lower shelf, and takes out the contents of the top shelf to
tidy it. The items consist of his scarf, the folding photograph frame, a
calendar, some exercise-books, a toy pistol and a model-car.*

RAINBOW, *carrying a buff-coloured O.H.M.S. envelope, enters up*
R, *leaving the door open*)

(*He is surprised*) I didn't ring for you.

RAINBOW (*moving* R *of the table* C; *aggrieved*) I never said you
did, Mr Billings.

BILLINGS (*aggressively*) Well, don't bring down young Sowter's
trunk, then.

RAINBOW (*offended*) I wasn't going to. (*He holds up the envelope*)
Letter for the Head.

BILLINGS. Oh.

RAINBOW (*jerking his head towards the door down* L) Is he in there?

BILLINGS. No. Out in the grounds. Better put it in there.

RAINBOW (*crossing to the door down* L, *looking at the envelope*)
O.H.M.S. Income Tax, it looks like.

BILLINGS. Well, he's in no mood for it now.

(RAINBOW *exits down* L. BILLINGS *has cleared his locker and stands
facing the audience, the contents of the locker clasped in his arms.*

MISS GOSSAGE *enters up* R. *Her face lights up as she sees
Billings*)

Gossage (*standing in the doorway; blithely*) Ah! Daisy!

(Billings *drops everything he is holding on to the floor*)

(*She moves down to* L *of Billings*) There! You are an old butter-fingers. I shall have to teach you to be tidy. Pick them up now.

(Rainbow *enters down* L. Billings, *giving Miss Gossage a bitter look, picks up the scarf and angrily throws it back in the locker. He misses and it falls to the floor again. As he stoops to pick up something else,* Miss Gossage *gives him a playful push and he lands on his hands and knees*)

(*To Billings, as to a child*) No, no—not like that. Let Sausage show you. (*She kneels* L *of him*)

(Billings, *with a bitter look, watches* Rainbow *crossing to the doors up* R.
Rainbow, *eyeing Billings with dry amusement, exits up* R, *closing the doors behind him. During this,* Miss Gossage, *on her knees, draws nearer to* Billings, *so that as he turns, their faces almost touch. He reacts, leaning back on the stool.* Miss Gossage *picks up the photograph frame and the calendar*)

(*She rises*) What a lot of useless odds and ends you seem to have collected.

Billings (*collecting the other items into a pile; dryly*) Yes—I want to avoid collecting any more.

Gossage (*putting the frame under her arm and looking at the calendar*) Look at this—last year's calendar—leap year, wasn't it?

Billings (*firmly*) Last year—yes. (*He takes the calendar from her, tears it up and throws the pieces in the waste-paper basket*)

Gossage. Of course, I think it's all bosh, anyway—about women proposing in leap year, don't you?

Billings (*relieved*) Oh, absolute bosh. (*He picks up the exercise-books and rises*)

Gossage (*moving close to him*) I mean—I don't see why they can't propose in any year—can you?

Billings (*recoiling*) Oh, no——

Gossage (*advancing*) Lots of men are simply head over heels in love and just don't realize it. (*She takes the exercise-books from him*)

Billings (*endeavouring to retreat further, but finding himself almost sitting on the table* R) Oh, yes, they do—I mean, no, they don't—I mean——

Gossage (*tenderly*) Daisy——

Billings (*desperately*) Look out. You'll drop that. (*He pushes the exercise-books out of her hand and they fall to the floor. He quickly bends down, gathers them up, along with the remaining items, and rams them all into his locker. The scarf is left where it fell*)

Gossage. I am in the awkward squad, aren't I? (*Coyly*) That was your fault. (*She fumbles with the photograph frame which comes open in her hands. She looks at it surprised*) Who are these four?

BILLINGS. Those—— (*He takes the frame and is about to put it in his locker, then stops, clutching at a straw*) Oh, these. Didn't I ever show you them?

(GOSSAGE *smilingly shakes her head as he crosses to* L *of her*)

(*He opens one fold of the frame*) That was my wife—Milly——

GOSSAGE (*dismayed*) Wife. I didn't know you were married once.

BILLINGS. Not once. (*He lets the other folds fall open*) Three times.

(GOSSAGE *reacts*)

(*Calmly*) That's the second one—Tilly. And that's my present wife, Lily. I expect to inherit a lot of money from her. Even more than I did from the other two.

GOSSAGE (*pointing to the last photograph; weakly*) Who—who's this one, then?

BILLINGS. Billie?—Oh, she's my fiancée—I'm going to marry her as soon as poor Lily pops off. (*Briskly*) Well, so long.

(BILLINGS *gives her the frame, smiles at her cheerfully, takes two dignified steps towards the doors up* R, *then in a sudden rush, exits and closes the doors behind him.* MISS GOSSAGE *stares aghast at the frame.*

MISS WHITCHURCH *and the* PECKS *enter through the french windows.* MISS WHITCHURCH *is wearing a mortar-board and academical gown, and has a whistle suspended on a black ribbon round her neck. She is carrying a rose.* MR PECK *has neither hat nor coat.* MISS GOSSAGE *puts the frame away in Billings' locker, then stands disconsolately leaning against the downstage end of the mantelpiece, facing the audience and staring into space*)

MR PECK (*moving down* L) But mathematics have always been Julia's weakest subject. It's quite miraculous—— (*To Mrs Peck*) Isn't it, dear?

MRS PECK (*moving down* LC; *quite innocently*) I think it's incredible.

WHITCHURCH (*moving below the table* C; *with a forced laugh*) That's hardly complimentary to our teaching staff. Is it, Miss Gossage? I'm sure Miss Gossage will tell you—just as I have—that—— (*She sees Miss Gossage's peculiar expression. Concerned*) Miss Gossage—you don't look yourself.

GOSSAGE (*faintly*) It's nothing, Miss Whitchurch—just the shock, that's all——

WHITCHURCH. Shock?

GOSSAGE. About Daisy—Mr Billings—being married three times.

(*The* PECKS *stare at her*)

WHITCHURCH. What?

MRS PECK. Three times?

GOSSAGE (*her indignation boiling over*) And only waiting for Lily to pop off before he does it again.

(*Overcome, she turns and exits with a dash up* R *closing the doors behind her. There is a momentary, shocked silence*)

MR PECK (*more in sorrow than in anger*) You see, Miss Whitchurch—this sort of environment—to a sensitive child——

WHITCHURCH (*pained*) You surely don't believe what you've just heard?

MRS PECK (*bewildered*) Shouldn't we?

WHITCHURCH (*firmly*) Of course not. Poor Miss Gossage. Overwork, you know. She's been having hallucinations.

MRS PECK. Hallucinations?

WHITCHURCH (*cheerfully confident*) Nothing at all to worry about. Just persecution and sex. (*She smells the rose pensively*) I'm having her thoroughly psycho-analysed—twice a week. That'll soon put a stop to it.

MR PECK. None the less——

WHITCHURCH. None the less, as you say, that is nothing to do with Julia. (*She puts the rose on the table* C) As I was telling you, her vulgar fractions have suddenly taken a turn for the better. As for her languages all this week—well, I simply can't tell you——

MR PECK (*impressed in spite of himself*) Really? I can't think why the child made no mention of it.

WHITCHURCH. A very modest girl.

MRS PECK (*suddenly remembering something*) But she said in her letter she got an *omega* for French—don't you remember, Edward?

MR PECK (*puzzled*) So she did.

WHITCHURCH. Quite impossible—I marked her myself. (*Brightly*) Of course that accounts for it. It's that wretched *alpha* of mine—always getting mistaken for my *omega*. (*Firmly*) No, no, I do assure you, Julia's really showing the most unexpected promise. (*Impressively*) I wonder what you'd say if I told you that there *are* such things as scholarships to Oxford——

MRS PECK. Miss Whitchurch—you're not suggesting——?

WHITCHURCH. Who knows? Early days yet. But I will say one thing—the air here seems to be working wonders——

MRS PECK (*impressed*) It seems almost a pity to take her out of it. (*To Mr Peck*) Doesn't it, Edward?

WHITCHURCH (*before Mr Peck can answer*) Oh, leave her. Let her breathe away for all she's worth. (*She turns up stage with her arms outflung towards the french windows*)

(*As the* PECKS *also turn,* BARBARA *peers in the doors up* R, *sees Miss Whitchurch and the Pecks and, with a sudden decision, enters. She carries a book with a lurid dust-jacket bearing the title "The Fruits of Passion")*

BARBARA. Oh, Miss Whitchurch—excuse me——
WHITCHURCH (*benevolently*) Yes, dear—what is it?
BARBARA (*moving down to Miss Whitchurch*) Just a book, Miss Whitchurch. Miss Harper asked me to bring it to her.
WHITCHURCH (*taking the book without looking at it*) Thank you, Barbara. Thank you, dear child. (*She turns to the Pecks*)

(BARBARA *exits up* R, *closing the doors behind her*)

There's another thing. St Swithins has always paid particular attention to general culture. We of the staff not only share their lessons, we share their pleasures too—help to mould their tastes during the most formative years. (*She gestures with the book*)

(MRS PECK *stares at the book*)

Miss Harper has quite a genius for interesting the girls in the right kind of literature——
MRS PECK (*in a strained voice*) Excuse me—— (*She takes the book from Miss Whitchurch, looks at it and passes it to Mr Peck. As she does so*) Edward.

(MR PECK *looks at the book, reacts in silence, and with it held gingerly between thumb and forefinger, crosses Mrs Peck and hands it to Miss Whitchurch. She looks at it, winces, and covering her face with one hand, holds the book behind her back with the other*)

WHITCHURCH (*in a strangled voice*) The Fruits of Passion——
MR PECK. I'm afraid, Miss Whitchurch, in the circumstances——
WHITCHURCH. I know what you're going to say, Mr Peck, but don't say it. Things aren't always what they seem.

(MR *and* MRS SOWTER *and* POND *enter through the french windows.* POND *looks worried and unhappy. They cross to* R, *passing between Miss Whitchurch and the table* C)

MR SOWTER (*indignantly*) You're telling me! Spend ten minutes looking for a mark, and when we find it, it's a fake. Whoever heard of a cricket ball with hobnails on it? (*He puts his hat and gloves on the table down* R)
MRS SOWTER. Unlikely.
MR SOWTER. Yes—and so's that story of Cyril hitting a six—— (*He glares at Pond*)
POND. I assure you, Mr Sowter——
MRS PECK (*looking at her watch*) Talking of six; it's nearly twenty past——

(MISS WHITCHURCH *and* POND *exchange a look and take a step towards each other*)

Mr Sowter. Twenty past?

Mr Peck (*to Miss Whitchurch*) Yes—I'm sorry, Miss Whitchurch, but we must go. (*He starts to move to the french windows*)

Whitchurch (*firmly*) Not without Julia's ration book. Come into the study, please. (*She crosses to the door down* L)

(Mr Peck *stops, turns, and exits down* L *with* Mrs Peck *and* Miss Whitchurch)

Mr Sowter (*to Pond; ferociously*) Where's my boy and his trunk?

Pond (*intimidated*) I'll see to it, Mr Sowter—I'll see the porter immediately.

(*He is about to move up* R, *when* Tassell *enters through the french windows*)

(*Relieved to see Tassell*) Ah—Tassell——

Tassell (*moving above the table* C) You haven't seen Miss Harper——?

Pond (*moving* R *of Tassell; exasperated*) Never mind Miss Harper. I was telling Mr Sowter about Cyril's cricket exploits—— (*With an attempt at jocularity*) But he seems to doubt my veracity. Now you tell him.

Tassell (*moving* R *of the table* C) Well, sir, I should like to say straight out that in my opinion your boy is the finest wicket-keeper we've ever had.

Mr Sowter (*crossing Mrs Sowter to* R *of Tassell*) Wicket-keeper? He was a bowler ten minutes ago. How the blazes can he do both at the same time?

Tassell (*retreating above the table* C; *weakly*) Well, he might have a sort of split personality.

Mr Sowter (*angrily*) Split my foot!

(Hopcroft *enters through the french windows, and moves* L *of the table* C)

Hopcroft (*to Pond*) Please, sir—Mr Sowter's taxi's here.

Pond (*aghast*) What?

Tassell (*moving* R *of Hopcroft*) Don't be silly, it can't be. (*To Pond. Anxiously*) Can it?

Pond. Not as far as I'm concerned.

Hopcroft. But it is, sir.

(Tassell *propels* Hopcroft *through the french windows*)

(*As he goes*) He says he's Mr Sowter's.

(Hopcroft *exits*)

Mr Sowter (*to Pond*) Are you going to speak to that porter, or aren't you?

POND. To tell you the truth, I'm not quite sure of his where-abouts.

MR SOWTER. If you can't find his whereabouts, *I* will. (*To Mrs Sowter*) Hilda. (*He leads the way purposefully up* R *and opens the doors*)

(MRS SOWTER *follows*)

You look upstairs—I'll look down—— (*He shouts*) Porter! Porter, blast you——

(MR SOWTER *exits to* R. MRS SOWTER *looks tentatively up the stairs, then goes up them and exits, leaving the doors open*)

POND (*to Tassell; defeatedly*) I think we've had it. (*He sinks into the chair above the table* C)

TASSELL (*moving to the doors up* R; *eagerly*) No, we haven't. If I can find Rainbow first, tell him to do a vanishing act ...

(TASSELL *exits hurriedly, closing the doors behind him.*
MISS WHITCHURCH *enters down* L)

WHITCHURCH (*speaking off; exasperatedly*) I'll find it, Mrs Peck —of course I will. Just wait, and *don't worry*.

MRS PECK (*off*) But——

(MISS WHITCHURCH *closes the door abruptly and turns to Pond. There is a look of desperation in her eye*)

WHITCHURCH (*moving* L *of Pond; a little breathlessly*) Julia's ration book. (*She produces it from under her gown*) It was in the drawer, but I managed to palm it. (*She puts the ration book on the table* C)

POND (*suspiciously*) Did you order a taxi?

WHITCHURCH. Certainly not.

POND. One's come.

WHITCHURCH. What!

POND. If the Sowters don't take it—the Pecks will.

WHITCHURCH (*forcefully*) Something must be done about it.

POND (*rising and moving* R *of the table* C; *despairingly*) What, for instance?

WHITCHURCH (*moving* L *of the table* C) I—I don't know—something drastic. (*An idea dawns*) Of course! If he did it, so can we.

POND. If who did what?

WHITCHURCH. Hopcroft. We'll puncture its back tyres.

POND. Back tyres?

WHITCHURCH (*impatiently*) The taxi's back tyres.

POND. We can't do that—it's—it's trespass or something.

WHITCHURCH. Desperate moments call for desperate measures. (*Urgently*) I wonder what he did it with?

POND. A penknife—but you won't go far with that.

WHITCHURCH (*desperately*) There must be something—some-where——

(*With an air of determination, MISS WHITCHURCH turns, puts her hands behind her back and, with her head bent in deep thought, hurries to the french windows. BILLINGS, entering, collides with her.*

MISS WHITCHURCH pivots completely round, but with her head still bent hurriedly exits)

BILLINGS (*moving above the table* C) What's happened now?
POND. A taxi's arrived. Someone's done the dirty.

(*MR SOWTER enters indignantly up* R, *pushing RAINBOW ahead of him, and followed by MRS SOWTER, who moves to the downstage end of the fireplace. RAINBOW has a boot he has been cleaning in one hand, and a boot brush in the other*)

MR SOWTER (*moving to the fireplace; to Pond, indignantly*) Found him, and what do I find? He says he was told *not* to bring it down.
POND (*to Rainbow*) Don't be ridiculous, Rainbow. Why should anyone tell you not to bring down a boy's trunk?
RAINBOW (*with an accusing look at Billings*) Mr Billings——

(*BILLINGS turns away and leans against the bookcase*)

POND (*sharply*) Rainbow. I want no excuses. Fetch down Master Sowter's trunk.
RAINBOW (*moving to the door up* R; *sulkily*) Yes, sir.
MR SOWTER. And tuck-box. (*He moves down* R)
RAINBOW (*on the verge of mutiny*) Yes, sir. (*He glares at Billings*)

(*TASSELL enters hurriedly through the french windows*)

TASSELL (*as he enters; to Pond, elatedly*) It may be all right. I couldn't find Rainbow—— (*He breaks off as he sees Rainbow*) Oh. The homo has missed the omnibus.

(*RAINBOW exits up* R, *closing the doors behind him.*

MR and MRS PECK enter down L. *MR PECK is carrying his hat and coat. TASSELL moves above the* R *end of the table* C)

MR PECK (*moving up* LC; *anxiously*) I'm sorry, but has anyone seen Miss Whitchurch?

(*MRS PECK follows MR PECK and stands* L *of him. MISS WHITCHURCH enters through the french windows. She is carrying a large axe, and has discarded her gown, but still wears her mortar-board*)

WHITCHURCH (*as she enters; triumphantly*) Here we are—I've got the very thing. (*She waves the axe, but pulls up with an exclamation of dismay as she sees the Pecks and Sowters*)

(*All stare at her*)

MR SOWTER. What the burning blazes are you doing with that?
WHITCHURCH (*to the Pecks; awkwardly*) I—er—had to break the safe open—for Julia's ration book.

Mrs Peck (*eagerly*) You have it, then?

(Mr Peck, *seeing the ration book on the table* c, *picks it up, and looks at the name on it*)

Whitchurch. Er—no. It wasn't in it.

Mr Peck. Wait a minute—it's here.

Whitchurch (*deflated*) Oh, is it?

Mr Peck (*waving the book triumphantly*) That's splendid. (*He puts it in his pocket*) I think we did hear our cab drive up.

Mrs Sowter (*formidably*) Ours.

Mr Sowter (*aggressively*) Don't you dare take that one.

Mr Peck (*throwing his hat and coat on the table* c) Really, sir—I've no desire to take your taxi——

Mrs Peck. We asked Miss Whitchurch to order one.

Tassell (*moving above the Pecks to* r *of Miss Whitchurch*) Oh, well, that won't be here, will it, Miss Whitchurch?

Whitchurch (*glaring*) I don't think so.

Tassell (*to the Pecks*) And then of course, there's *your* luggage.

(Barbara *enters up* r, *leaving the door open, and moves to the upstage* r *corner of the table* c)

Barbara. Excuse me, Miss Whitchurch—but we've brought down Julia's trunk and things——

(Pond *on her right and* Billings *on her left seem to close in on her threateningly*)

Whitchurch. What! Who has? (*She raises the axe as if to strike someone*)

Barbara (*looking askance at the axe*) Some of the other girls and me. We couldn't find Rainbow anywhere, and we didn't want them to miss the train.

(Barbara *beams in an artlessly friendly way, turns and exits up* r, *closing the door behind her*)

Whitchurch (*acidly*) Dear, thoughtful child. I must remember to give her a mark of some kind. (*She looks at the axe meaningly*)

Tassell (*moving above Miss Whitchurch to* l *of her*) It's sabotage—that's what it is—sabotage.

Mr Sowter (*angrily*) Nothing but inefficiency! Their trunk and no taxi. Our taxi and no trunk.

Billings (*with a gesture of helplessness*) There's life for you. (*He moves up* r)

Mr Sowter. Two minutes, and we'll go without the trunk.

Mr Peck (*moving below the table* c; *timidly*) In that case, perhaps you could sandwich us in——

Mr Sowter (*explosively*) Sandwich you! I'll see you in . . .

Mrs Sowter. Edgar!

Mr Sowter. Eh?

Mrs Sowter. Clergyman.

Mr Sowter. Oh. (*Reluctantly*) Well—yes—all right. (*He moves to the table down* R *and starts impatiently flipping over the pages of the magazines on it*)

(Billings *eases to* R *of the table* c)

Whitchurch. Pond. Are you going to stand there and accept defeat?

Pond (*moving below the* R *end of the table* c; *desperately*) Mr Sowter —Mrs Sowter—Mr and Mrs Peck—I appeal to you—for the sake of your boy and girl. Think of your own schooldays—the happiest days of your life—— ~~& QUICK~~

Mr Sowter. Nonsense.

Tassell. Well, if you'd spent them here, perhaps they might have been.

Pond. After all, what harm's been done.

Mr Sowter (*furiously*) What harm? Turning my boy into a little . . .

Billings (*before Mrs Sowter can speak*) Edgar!

(*The* Sowters *glare at him*. Pond *and* Billings *react to each other*. Tassell, *to conceal his laughter, moves to* R *of the french windows*)

Pond (*to Mr Peck*) I put it to you, sir. Look at—look at Noah's Ark. They went into that two by two——

(Mr Sowter *turns back to the table down* R, *sees the misconduct mark-book, picks it up and looks at it*)

Mr Peck. Possibly, but not for educational purposes.

Whitchurch (*shocked*) Mr Peck, if you're suggesting——

Mr Sowter (*moving* R *of Pond with the misconduct book*) No harm done, he says. Look at this. A book full of misconduct.

Mrs Sowter. Misconduct?

Mr Sowter (*reading the cover label*) "St Swithins School, Misconduct Marks." (*Outraged*) Why, dammit, they even give marks for it. (*To Mrs Sowter*) Come on, Hilda, we're going. (*He moves back to the table down* R)

Pond (*crossing to the door down* L; *desperately*) No, no, you can't. Not without Cyril's ration book.

(Pond *exits down* L. Billings *moves quickly to Mr Sowter and takes the book from him*)

Billings. You've got it all wrong, sir. You've only got to read the entries. All perfectly innocent. (*He opens the book and reads*) "Eleanor Gribble—refused to eat gribble"——

Whitchurch (*with umbrage*) The word is gristle.

Billings (*looking at the entry*) So it is, I'm sorry. (*He reads*) "Julia Peck"—— (*He smiles at the Pecks*) Ah, Julia Peck—"left her chisel on the floor." (*With asperity*) Oh, so that's who it was. (*He perches himself on the down* R *corner of the table* C *and rubs his heel*)

(TASSELL *moves above the table* C)

(*He reads*) "Peggy Hobson—caught in dormitory with the Four Just Men——" (*He turns to Tassell with raised eyebrows*) Oh, I see. (*He reads*) "Daphne Carruthers——"

MR SOWTER (*angrily*) Are you trying to waste our time?

BILLINGS. Yes. I mean no—— (*He throws the book on to the table* C)

MR SOWTER (*picking up his hat and gloves and moving to the doors up* R) We're going, then.

MR PECK. So are we. (*He picks up his hat and coat and starts to move to the doors up* R)

MR SOWTER (*to Billings*) Tell Pond to put the ration book in the trunk and send it on.

(MRS PECK *and* MRS SOWTER *follow their husbands up* R.

As the four reach the doors up R, POND *enters hurriedly down* L, *waving a letter in one hand, and the buff envelope in the other*)

POND (*moving below the table* C) It's come! It's come! In the nick of time!

BILLINGS (*puzzled*) Your Income Tax?

POND. Income Tax? No, no—it's from the Ministry.

TASSELL. Fraphampton? (*He moves down* L *of Miss Whitchurch*)

WHITCHURCH. Devacuation? (*She eases* L *of Pond*)

POND. Yes, yes! Oh, never again will I speak rudely of the Civil Service. (*He reads excitedly*) "In answer to your communications, dated so and so and so and so, I am directed to inform you that from Saturday next . . ." (*He looks up*) That's today. (*He resumes reading*) "Your premises will no longer be shared by St Swithins——"

(*There are general murmurs of delight and relief. The* SOWTERS *and* PECKS *ease to above the upstage* R *corner of the table* C)

(*He reads*) "only, but also . . ." (*He looks mystified, turns back, and re-reads to get the sense right*) "no longer be shared by St Swithins only, but also by another homeless institution—the Meadowvale Academy for Backward Boys and Forward Girls, whose two hundred and fifty pupils will be arriving on the tenth inst." (*He looks up, gasping*) That's this inst!

(*All stand dumbfounded.* MISS GOSSAGE *hurries in agitatedly up* R, *leaving the doors open*)

GOSSAGE (*running down* R; *breathlessly*) Miss Whitchurch! There's oodles and oodles of buses coming in—full of screaming children——

POND (*frantically*) No, no, they can't! They mustn't!

WHITCHURCH. They will, if we don't stop them.
TASSELL. Then what are we waiting for?
WHITCHURCH. Come on then. (*She hands the axe to Pond*) Bolt the doors, bar the windows. Barricade them.

(MISS WHITCHURCH *and* MISS GOSSAGE *dash to the french windows to close and bolt them.*

TASSELL *runs to the doors up* R *and exits.*

MRS SOWTER *moves above the table* C, *takes off her gloves, and puts them, with her handbag, on the table* C. MR PECK *puts his mackintosh over his arm, and moves the chair above the table* C *to* R *of the bookcase, then moves behind the chair* L *of the table* C. MRS PECK *moves to the* L *end of the table* C, *taking off her gloves as she does so*)

POND. I'm going to ring the Ministry.

(RAINBOW *comes downstairs, carrying a tuck-box on his shoulder and dragging a trunk*)

BILLINGS. Closed till Monday. (*He pulls the chair* R *of the table* C *down stage a little, sits, and unconcernedly starts to light a pipe*)
POND (*desperately*) The Cabinet, then—I don't know—— (*He crosses to the table down* R, *almost tripping over Billings' legs*)

(MISS GOSSAGE *closes the* R *half of the french windows,* MISS WHITCHURCH *the* L *half, and holds both while* MISS GOSSAGE *tries to reach the upper bolt which is too high for her. The* SOWTERS *and* PECKS *look at each other indecisively*)

MR SOWTER (*to the Pecks; aggressively*) Well, don't stand there —lend a hand, can't you?

(MR SOWTER *takes hold of the* L *end of the table* C, MRS SOWTER *the upstage* R *corner of it.* MRS PECK *moves below the table* C, *puts her gloves, handbag and umbrella on it and takes hold of the downstage edge.* MR PECK *carries the chair from* L *of the table* C *to near the door down* L, *then returns, takes hold of the* L *end of the table* C *and helps* MR SOWTER *to carry it to the french windows.* MISS GOSSAGE *promptly climbs on to the table, to reach the bolt.* MISS WHITCHURCH, *who is bending to fasten the lower bolt, is hemmed in between the table and the french windows.*

TASSELL *appears up* R, *and meets* RAINBOW *at the foot of the stairs.* TASSELL *grabs the tuck-box, enters the room and puts the tuck-box on the chair by the bookcase*)

RAINBOW (*indignantly*) What's the idea?

(RAINBOW *enters the room up* R)

TASSELL (*shouting over the tumult*) Bring down twenty more. (*He moves to the table down* R)
RAINBOW (*outraged*) Blimey! (*He gets the trunk and puts it in the room* L *of the doors up* R)

(*The front-door bell starts to ring off, and the noise is increased by the sound of the knocker*)

TASSELL (*picking up the scarf and the waste-paper basket, and shouting to Rainbow*) Don't answer that.

RAINBOW (*shouting back rebelliously*) I wasn't going to. (*He runs to the foot of the stairs and shouts*) Hi, kids, bring down all them trunks in the box-room. (*He waits at the foot of the stairs*)

(POND *seats himself on the stool down* R, *lifts the telephone receiver and dials.* MISS WHITCHURCH *crawls out from underneath the table, getting entangled in the table-cloth as she does so.* MRS SOWTER *takes her bag and gloves off the table, puts them on the bookcase ledge, crosses to the table up* R, *and puts the globe from off it, on to the floor.* MR SOWTER *picks up the misconduct book and rose from the table, moves to the doors up* R, *gives the rose to Rainbow and flings the book into the upstage* R *corner.* MR PECK *hangs his mackintosh and hat on the pegs* L, *then helps* MRS PECK *to push the easy chair* L *against the* L *end of the table.* MISS GOSSAGE *jumps down from the table, and moving to the trunk by the doors up* R, *endeavours to to drag it* L)

GOSSAGE (*to Billings; frantically*) Mr Billings, *do* something.

(BILLINGS *hardly troubles even to look at her, and continues to attend to his pipe.*

JOYCE *enters up* R *and leans against the door-post, surveying the scene in horror.* POND *still dials frantically and ineffectually.* TASSELL *puts the scarf and waste-paper basket on the table down* R, *lifts up the telephone instrument and transfers it to* POND'S *knees.* POND *rises to put the instrument back on the table.* TASSELL *forthwith picks up the stool and puts that on the table.* POND *puts the instrument on the stool.* TASSELL *takes it off and hands it, with the scarf, which has got entwined, to* POND, *who now gets completely entangled with the scarf, telephone cord and the receiver. With the stool and the waste-paper basket balanced on top,* TASSELL *picks up the table, turns and staggers* L. *As he does so* JOYCE *moves down* C. TASSELL *smiles at* JOYCE, *turning a complete circle as he does so, then staggers on and deposits his load at the french window barricade.* JOYCE *goes to try to help* POND, *but he shoos her away.*

MISS WHITCHURCH, *having got out of the table-cloth, rises to her feet, thinks of something and exits hurriedly down* L.

BARBARA *and* HOPCROFT *now appears on the stairs and pass trunks and suitcases down to* RAINBOW, *who dumps them inside the room* L *of the doors up* R. MR SOWTER *pushes the easy chair from* R *over to the barricade, then assisted by* MISS GOSSAGE *lifts the trunks and suitcases on to the table by the window.* MRS SOWTER *carries the table from up* R *and dumps it in the easy chair. She then helps with the trunks and suitcases.* MR PECK *also gives a hand.* MRS PECK *carries the small chair from down* L *and adds it to the stack at the windows.*

MISS WHITCHURCH, *carrying an air-gun, enters down* L, *moves to the barricade, mounts the small chair and aims the airgun towards the french windows, as though to repel invaders. MRS PECK busies herself stacking the waste-paper basket and other small items on to the table. The school bell is now heard being rung off, adding to the din being made by the front-door bell and knocker. TASSELL, returning from the barricade, meets Joyce C. With sudden determination, he stops and, inaudible owing to the uproar, asks her to marry him. JOYCE gives a delighted nod of assent and they go into each other's arms. BILLINGS goes on unconcernedly smoking his pipe as the CURTAIN falls, only to rise again immediately. The action continues. Trunks and suitcases are still being passed and stacked. POND is just managing to disentangle himself. JOYCE and TASSELL are embracing and BILLINGS is still quietly seated smoking his pipe. Suddenly, MISS WHITCHURCH jumps down from the chair, puts her airgun down, moves down C, turns her back to the audience, and blows a blast on her whistle. The school bell and the door bell stop ringing. The knocker stops. All stop what they are doing and gather round MISS WHITCHURCH. After a moment she calls)*

WHITCHURCH. Disperse. *(She turns slowly to face the audience)*

As she does so, all move to their call positions as follows. (From L to R) HOPCROFT, RAINBOW, MRS SOWTER, MR SOWTER, MISS GOSSAGE, BILLINGS, MISS WHITCHURCH, POND, JOYCE, TASSELL, MRS PECK, MR PECK, BARBARA. *They bow as—*

the CURTAIN *falls*

FURNITURE AND PROPERTY LIST

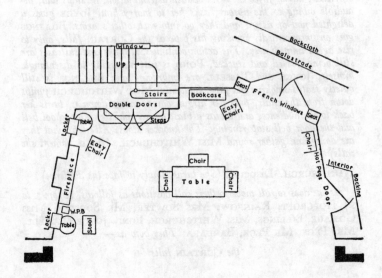

ACT I

Throughout the play:

On stage—Small table (down R). *On it:* Telephone with long lead. Magazines.
Ashtray
Waste-paper basket
Stool
Locker (down R). *In it:* Boxing-gloves, stick of pink mint rock
2 easy chairs
Small table (up R). *On it:* Globe of the world
Locker (up R). *In it:* Mortar-board (*dusty*), gown (*dusty*)
Refectory table
2 elbow chairs
2 dining chairs
Bookcase. *In it:* Books, including school directory
        On it: 2 silver cups
        On ledge: Ashtray
On mantelpiece—Black marble clock, 2 bronze figures with candles,
cigarette-box, tobacco jar
In fireplace—Brass fender
        Fire-irons
        Decoration in grate
Rug in front of fireplace
Pair of dark curtains
Pair of net curtains (*concealed for Act I under the dark curtains*)

98

Ashtray on window seat
4 hat pegs. *On them:* POND's mortar-board
On wall above mantelpiece—Old picture of Victorian gentleman
On wall above door L—Map of the world
Carpet on floor
In the hall—Small table
> *On window-sill:* School bell
> *On wall:* Notice board

Off stage—Cricket bag (TASSELL). *In it:* Cricket bat, cricket pads, cricket gloves,
> cricket boots
> Suitcase (TASSELL)
> Tennis balls in net bag (TASSELL)
> Tennis racquet in press (TASSELL)
> Golf bag with clubs (TASSELL)
> Mortar-board and gown (BILLINGS)
> 7 books (BILLINGS)
> Hilary Hall scarf (10 feet long) (BILLINGS)
> 4-fold photograph frame containing photographs of 4 middle-aged
> > ladies (BILLINGS)
> 2 large parcels of books (RAINBOW)
> Duster (RAINBOW)
> Green baize apron (RAINBOW)
> White apron (RAINBOW)
> Tennis racquet in press (BARBARA)
> Camera in case (BARBARA)
> Suitcase (BARBARA)
> Joyce Harper's jacket (BARBARA)
> Joyce Harper's mackintosh (BARBARA)
> Stamped letter (BARBARA)
> Book (POND)
> Attaché case (MISS WHITCHURCH)
> Foolscap list (MISS WHITCHURCH)
> Kit-bag (MISS GOSSAGE)
> Haversack (MISS GOSSAGE)
> Letter from Ministry (POND)
> Telegram (POND)
> Notebook (POND)
> School lists (POND)
> Letter from MRS SOWTER (POND)
> List of accommodation, 3″ × 4″ (POND)

Personal—TASSELL: Pencil, cigarette-case with cigarettes, lighter, 2 half-crowns
> BILLINGS: Ten-shilling note
> BARBARA: School satchel
> MISS WHITCHURCH: Gloves, umbrella, handbag. *In it:* handkerchief,
> > brooch watch
> MISS GOSSAGE: Spectacles

At end of act:

Strike—Everything off table C
> Everything off mantelpiece
> Mortar-boards and gowns off pegs L
> Decoration from grate
> Fireplace rug
> Magazines from table down R
> All ashtrays

Re-set furniture—Table C up and down stage
> Easy chair from up LC to L
> Chair from L to LC

Set—*On top of lockers:* Bronze figures from mantelpiece
    On table down R: 3 women's coloured magazines
    In locker down R: Calendar, exercise-books, 4-fold photograph frame, scarf,
        toy pistol, toy motor-car, school lists
    On mantelpiece: Ormulu clock, 2 Japanese china vases, 2 tall vases
    In firegrate: Beech-leaves in brown jug
    In front of fireplace: Patterned rug
    In locker up R: Cricket boots, 3 books, tennis balls in net bag
    In corner up R: Cricket bat
    In hall: Patterned rug.
            Notice board with vertical white tape
    On top of bookcase: 3 small silver cups, labels
    On floor LC: Coloured rug
    By door down L: Patterned rug
    On table C: Brown chenille table-cloth
            Blue vase. *In it:* "Old Man's Beard" and "Queen Anne's Lace"
    Piece of india-rubber
    2 piles of stamped envelopes with letters in them
    On chair LC: Cushion
    On floor R *of chair* LC: Flat work-basket. *In it:* Pair of pyjamas with frills,
        pair of very feminine knickers, nightdress, mark-book, pencil.
    In easy chair L: Exercise-books
                Pencil
                2 cushions
    In easy chair R: 2 cushions
    On window seats: Cushions
    Reveal net curtains at french windows
    Replace map of world by poster picture

ACT II

Off stage—School lists (TASSELL)
        Pile of unstamped envelopes with letters in them (JOYCE)
        Boys' magazine (HOPCROFT)
        Netball goal-post (RAINBOW)
        Golden Syrup tin (MISS WHITCHURCH)
        Bunch of turquoise larkspur (BARBARA)
        Small parcel (MRS PECK)
        Box of chocolates (MR PECK)
        Daily Telegraph (MR PECK)
        Garden hoe (BARBARA)
        Old glove (BARBARA)
        Personal—MR PECK: Raincoat, gloves, hat
        MRS PECK: Handbag, umbrella, gloves
        TASSELL: Cigarette-case with cigarettes, lighter, fountain-pen
        MISS GOSSAGE: Wrist-watch
        BILLINGS: Fountain-pen, 2 half-crowns
        HOPCROFT: 1 half-crown
        MR SOWTER: Hat, gloves   letter
        MRS SOWTER: Gloves, handbag

At end of act:

Strike—Everything from table C except cloth
        Vase of flowers from mantelpiece
        Flowers from waste-paper basket

Re-set furniture—Table C across stage

Set—*On table down* R: Misconduct mark-book
                Typed Ministry letter

ACT III

Off stage—Note, from Mrs Hampstead (HOPCROFT)
O.H.M.S. envelope (*sealed*) (RAINBOW)
Tuck-box (RAINBOW)
Book, *Fruits of Passion* (BARBARA)
7 trunks
4 suitcases
Rose (MISS WHITCHURCH)
Axe (MISS WHITCHURCH)
Blue ration book (MISS WHITCHURCH)
O.H.M.S. letter and envelope (*open*) (POND)
Airgun (MISS WHITCHURCH)
Boot (RAINBOW)
Boot brush (RAINBOW)

Personal—MISS WHITCHURCH: Whistle on black ribbon
POND: Handkerchief
RAINBOW: Pencil, paper
MISS GOSSAGE: Watch
MR SOWTER: Watch
MRS PECK: Watch
BILLINGS: Pipe, pouch with tobacco, matches

MADE AND PRINTED IN GREAT BRITAIN BY
LATIMER TREND & COMPANY LTD PLYMOUTH